Thanks for joining
us this evening. This
has been a special night
in a special community.
Enjoy the book!
Best —
Bynthack

DOWN BY THE RIVER

DOWN BY THE RIVER

From Colorado
to the Mississippi Delta

A Cultural Adventure in
Teaching, Coaching,
and Learning

BRYCE HACH

SEABOARD PRESS

JAMES A. ROCK & COMPANY, PUBLISHERS

Down by the River: From Colorado to the Mississippi Delta,
A Cultural Adventure in Teaching, Coaching, and Learning by Bryce Hach

SEABOARD PRESS

is an imprint of JAMES A. ROCK & CO., PUBLISHERS

Down by the River: From Colorado to the Mississippi Delta,
A Cultural Adventure in Teaching, Coaching, and Learning
copyright ©2009 by Bryce Hach

Special contents of this edition copyright ©2009 by Seaboard Press

Address comments and inquiries to:
SEABOARD PRESS
900 South Irby Street, #508
Florence, South Carolina 29501

E-Mail:
jrock@rockpublishing.com   lrock@rockpublishing.com
Internet URL: www.rockpublishing.com

Trade Paperback ISBN-13/EAN: 978-1-59663-576-0

Library of Congress Control Number: 2007930606

Printed in the United States of America

First Edition: 2009

Dedicated to

all teachers

in America

After parenting,

you have

the most important

job in the world

Acknowledgments

There are many wonderful people I need to thank who made this book possible. Many warm thanks go out to ...

Christa Gieszl, for first introducing me to the idea of Teach For America.

Alex Quigley, Amy Sudmyer, Joanna Hass, Kristi Smith, John Friedberg and William Quin, for being wonderful friends and soundboards of empathy, as you went through the same experience.

Jim and Micki Cassidy, for introducing me to the true meaning of Southern hospitality.

Shirely Rotenberry, for being a consummate supporter and friend.

Aaron Holden, for the lifelong memories.

The wonderful people of Quitman County, for letting me be a part of your lives.

Alison Stewart, for editing this memoir.

My sisters, Heather and Haley, for being loving friends.

My parents, Bruce and Muriel, because being a teacher highlighted just how overwhelmingly important you both were to my upbringing.

Sarah, my loving wife, for supporting me through the writing of this memoir from its very inception.

Contents

Instead of making a real investment in education that could pay itself back many times, our society has chosen to pay the price three times: once, when we let the kids through the educational system; twice, when they drop out to a street life of poverty, dependence and maybe even crime; and a third time when we warehouse those who have crossed over the line and gotten caught. The cost of this neglect is immense, in dollars and in abuse of the human spirit. We must educate our children.

—The Honorable Alan Page, Minnesota Supreme Court
    Justice and NFL Defensive End during his Pro
    Football Hall of Fame enshrinement speech

Don't try to make life a mathematics problem with yourself in the middle and everything coming out equal. When you are good, bad things can still happen and if you are bad, you can still get lucky.

—Barbara Kingsolver's novel *The Poisonwood Bible*

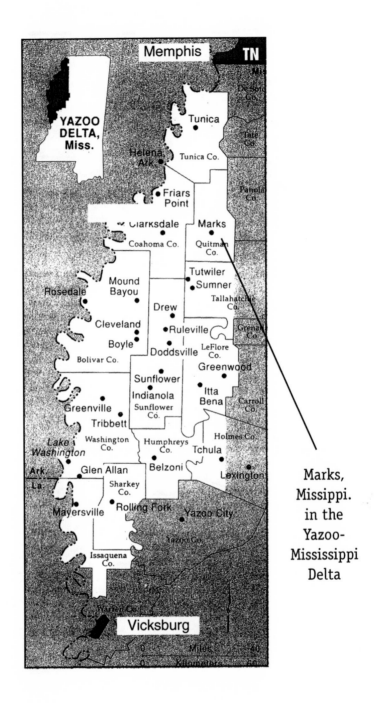

Marks, Missippi. in the Yazoo-Mississippi Delta

CHAPTER 1

What on Earth
Am I Doing Here?

I've had experiences that were this absurd and bizarre before, but there was always an alarm clock a few hours away to reunite me with my life. This time, no clock.

It was a warm, humid September night in a cotton field. The sun was setting quickly. Enveloped in the sound of cicadas and my own heartbeat, sweat swelling and running down my body, I picked up my step as I ran. I was looking for a main road, a road that might have traffic. Traffic meant cars, and cars meant an opportunity to hitchhike. If I was going to get home this evening, a car was my only hope.

I ran for three reasons. The first was the approaching darkness. Without knowing where I was, finding the main road in an incredibly rural area was tough enough. At night, that search was nearly impossible. Second, the mosquitoes

1

waited anxiously to bite if I slowed. Biting insects have always had a fondness for me, and in the Mississippi Delta, my body became a buffet for the masses. A walk or even a slow jog meant a feeding frenzy and as they preyed upon me, I did not want to be eaten. Third, I was not alone. Four high school football players were with me. They were my responsibility. I was their coach.

After almost twenty minutes of running through the cotton field, I found a main road. Out of exhaustion, the players and I put our hands on top of our heads and took deep breaths of air. After a few minutes, two car lights began to zoom in from the distance. With our thumbs ready and smiles on our faces to look amiable, probably both unnoticeable in the darkness of the growing night, a minivan stopped for us. We piled our smelly bodies into the back seat. The driver asked us what happened. I told him.

I had already been at school teaching and then coaching football for twelve hours when I got behind the wheel of the small school bus to drive the boys home from practice. None of our players had cars and, as a county high school, they lived in one of six different towns spread out between cotton fields and bayous.

Still with a whistle around my neck, I pulled open the creaky yellow, heavy-duty door and climbed into the driver's seat. I had never driven a school bus until a few weeks ago and, after my short experience with it, I'd have happily parted ways.

The school bus was horribly ancient. Holes on the bottom presented the road running under my feet and the bus headlights offered little visual safety after the sun went down. Most driving took place on dusty dirt roads, far from civilization. Our players lived in remote locations that required crossing rickety bridges that I had thought only existed in scary children's fairy tales. As the bus slowly edged forward across each bridge, I gripped tightly to the steering wheel and my players gripped their seats in case we fell through into the river basin below.

In concert with the bus, the players' behavior constantly teetered on bedlam. Pinching, hitting, swearing, and rude jokes swirled around me as I searched for new forms of discipline. As a raw, first-year teacher, I found classroom management an hourly, if not minute-by-minute, concern. Occasionally, I stopped the bus on the side of the road and warned them they would be walking home unless their behavior befit their ages.

On this particular evening, their behavior was much improved, but the bus itself was in poor shape. With many of the players already dropped off, about thirty minutes into the drive, fumes of smoke rose from under the hood and brushed threateningly against my insect-carcass-laden windshield. About two minutes later, the bus stopped altogether. One of my players said, "Oh shit! What now, Coach?"

I looked forward through the smoke, which was seeping into the bus, at the silhouette of cotton plants and trees across the tableland. I said, "First of all, I'm not a fan of hearing you guys swear. Secondly, I think we have a real problem here."

I got out of the bus and opened the hood. Without a lid, hot, bubbling antifreeze boiled off the top of the engine. A couple drops spit out on my arm and burned on my skin. Wiping my arm with my shirt, I told the players we needed to find another means of transportation. I asked them where the nearest main road was. They all instinctively pointed across the cotton field.

"Okay, then that is where we need to go," I said. We all got our things out of the bus, abandoned it, and started with a slow jog.

* * *

After the kind man in the minivan dropped everyone off, I called the principal and relayed the situation. I did not even know where I'd abandoned the bus.

"Somewhere off in the cotton fields near Falcon," I told the principal. I took a quick shower, grabbed an apple out of the refrigerator and looked at the clock. "Oh, shit!" I said to myself out loud. I had to be back at the school to teach in seven hours.

I was a high school teacher and football coach in the Mississippi Delta, four months out of college. Initially, I'd felt Teach For America gave the Mississippi Delta to me. As it turns out, they gave me to the Mississippi Delta.

CHAPTER 2

Esprit de Corps

I grew up in a small town along the front range of the Rocky Mountains in Loveland, Colorado. As a child, I remember a poster that circulated around town displaying a young couple arm-in-arm, overlooking Lake Loveland, with the mountains reflecting off the water and a hot air balloon overhead that said simply "Life is Good in Loveland!" Every year, thousands of people around the country send their Valentine's cards to be postmarked through America's "Sweetheart City." In Loveland's history, among the main industries were the cherry farms in the hills and the sugar plant in the city. In more recent times, Loveland has been economically fueled with the help of high tech firms and booming retail.

Loveland was good to me and my little world hummed along at a gentle but healthy pace. In Loveland, I discovered sports and girls, survived the awkward middle-school years of acne and self-doubt, became the captain and quarterback of the Loveland High School football team, the student body president, and the prom king.

In Loveland, I fell in love with education. In high school, I coached a little-league soccer team and student taught elementary school children in nature classes up in the mountains during field trips. Based on my limited experience interacting with youth, I felt I wanted to become a teacher someday.

I went to a small liberal arts school two hours down the road, Colorado College, in Colorado Springs. By mid-spring 1998, I was all but finished with college, ready to fulfill my dreams of going into education.

The last few weeks of college are frequently a time to simply relax and enjoy some fleeting moments with friends made over the previous four years before entering the job market. However, I was edgy for information. Each day, I nervously walked to my student center college mailbox and frantically flipped the dial of my lock, only to find it empty or filled with mail of lesser priority. I was waiting to hear back from the admissions people at Teach For America.

About a month earlier, I'd had my interview. The interviewers told us we would hear back in three weeks if we had been accepted. When three weeks came and went, I could not take any more anticipation. I called the Teach For America office in New York and asked if I had been accepted. The woman on the phone simply told me to wait for the mail. I took this as a bad sign. My intuition told me that, if I was accepted, they would have just told me, whereas a rejection could be done nicely with the distance of mail.

During the interview in Denver, we were asked to read and discuss some pertinent articles on education issues, complete a five-minute individual lesson of our choice, and participate in a one-on-one interview. I chose to do a mildly humorous fifth-grade-level lesson about tornadoes, based mostly on information I found in a National Geographic video. I scrutinized and rehearsed the lesson a number of times, both to friends and to myself, making sure I maximized my five minutes.

As I waited in the lobby for my individual interview, sitting beneath a "Teach For America" banner, I picked up a copy of their monthly newsletter, *Esprit de Corps*. The magazine featured articles about smiling Teach For America teachers and photos of students with hands in the air, anxious to answer and learn. The images gave me a curious "Norman Rockwell" feeling of teaching where everything is both happy and good.

Finally, on a warm sunny day in May, about a week before graduation, a small envelope with the Teach For America logo lay in my Colorado College mailbox #345. I walked out of the student center and sat down on a campus bench where I nervously opened the envelope.

Upon reading the envelope's contents, I quickly realized two things. First, I had been accepted by Teach For America. Second, I was going to live in the Mississippi Delta. Although I was very excited, the bit about the Mississippi Delta was a question mark. I could not even pinpoint where that region was—I guessed it must be in Mississippi, but I'd thought the delta of the Mississippi River was in Louisiana, where the river dumped into the Gulf of Mexico.

I had zero experience with this state. I'd never been there, and the only real things I knew about Mississippi were that it was in the Deep South, its capital is Jackson (thanks to a still-remembered eighth grade social studies class lesson), and it was a pivotal state in the Civil Rights Movement. Other than that, all I had was a set of naïve assumptions about speaking with southern drawls, eating grits, waving Confederate flags, and drinking sweet tea on a porch under the shade of Spanish moss.

Regardless, I would learn about all those things later, in their own time. Now, it was a call for celebration. I bounced off the bench and called my friends and family to tell them that I was moving to Mississippi.

After receiving the accolades from friends and family over the phone, I was still hot on the idea of Mississippi. Later that afternoon, I walked over to the Colorado College library with a mission to look up anything I could find about Mississippi. I scrolled down the library search engine for "Mississippi" and on the second page, I found a PBS civil rights video titled, *"Mississippi: Is This America?"*

Finding the VHS video, I went to the check-out desk. I picked up a pair of headphones, purchased a bag of Gummi Bears and Coca-Cola from the vending machine and proceeded to the basement-level television viewing cubicles. In my darkened cubicle, I opened the bag of Gummi Bears and watched grainy black and white images of African Americans living out of dilapidated shacks and being driven down streets with fire hoses. I watched Medgar Evers' body being carted off his own front lawn and hateful speeches by men in finely tailored suits representing the White Citizens Council.

I knew this may have been the Mississippi of forty years ago, but certainly not the state in which I was going to live.

A week or so later, I graduated from college and was living with my parents back in Loveland for a couple weeks.

*CHECK ON A CONFESSION OF A White WOMAN, IN REFERENCE TO MegAR EVAN's Whistling At her.

I received a second letter from Teach For America stating I would be teaching in the town of Marks in Quitman County. My high school was M.S. Palmer, named after a previous principal.

I got out the "M" volume from *World Book Encyclopedia* in the living room and looked up Marks on the Mississippi state map. About 60 miles south of Memphis, Marks was nowhere near the delta of the Mississippi River. The dot on the map gave license to my imagination and I pictured alligators, the Klu Klux Klan, and wooded roads leading to huge plantations.

A couple weeks later, I was finally ready to start this adventure. I packed my things into my Volkswagen for the Teach For America Summer Institute in Houston, Texas, a teacher training program. I bid my parents good-bye, hugged the two Cocker Spaniels, the Yorkshire Terrier, and my cat, Thomas. With tears in my eyes, I started the car and got on the interstate, heading south.

For the first two hours of my drive to Houston, it felt like just another trip back to school following a weekend at home. However, as I passed my college exit, I began traveling on unfamiliar highways and my new reality took shape. A short stint in Houston was all that separated me from everything I'd ever known, and a life I could only imagine.

* * *

In Houston, the Teach For America Summer Institute was a whirlwind. In six weeks, the 700 corps members embarked upon quite a journey, transforming recent college graduates into bona fide teachers. The summer was an arduous educators' boot camp, preparing us for our differing roads ahead.

I met many wonderful people. One went to teach kindergarten in the South Bronx, a short walk from Yankee Stadium, where she had to overcome four different languages in the same classroom, giant cockroaches that spread asthma, and abject urban poverty. Another left for rural North Carolina where she lived in the backside of a family corner store and taught middle school North Carolina history, the state she had just moved to, and coached the girls' basketball team. All of us had unique stories to tell.

Upon completing the Summer Institute, I set off on Highway 10, along the Gulf of Mexico, for the Delta. Over the bayou causeways, I opened my car's sunroof, took in the warm, humid, late-July Gulf air and played Paul Simon's song *Graceland*. The song begins with the lyrics, "The Mississippi Delta was shining like a national guitar ..."

On the road, evening began to fall. I stopped off for a chicken sandwich and cherry limeade at a Sonic Drive-In near Baton Rouge and then turned onto a road that would soon become familiar; Highway 61 bisects the Delta vertically. As I drove, a night rainstorm caught up with my speeding car. Then in the distance, I saw a big white sign approaching through the intermittent clarity of the windshield wipers. The sign read, "Mississippi, The Hospitality State Welcomes You," with a big magnolia flower draped across the top. Without even a momentary hesitation, I rolled down my car window and stuck out my head. As the rain hit my face, it felt like a baptism. I howled into the night air with joy.

Finally, I was in Mississippi. I'd wanted something outside my Colorado life and, through Teach For America, I'd found it.

CHAPTER 3

Race
and History

In Colorado, I never got much flavor for local history.
Sure, I went to the Loveland Museum a number of times
and saw the nice displays of early frontier life, the old
Loveland sugar plant exhibit, and the photo display of past
Miss Loveland Valentines, the Loveland teenage beauty
queen. But it never enraptured me much emotionally.

Since our family first moved to Loveland in the early
1980's, so much of the city had completely changed. New
developments sprouted every year: outlet malls, multiplex
movie theaters, and housing developments with fancy marketed names like "Seven Lakes," "Enchantment Ridge," or
"Golden Harvest."

The fresh, clean newness of northern Colorado at times
felt sterile—new houses with new walls, which hadn't gathered many secrets. Even the people are new; most

Coloradoans are either first or second generation, drawing primarily from places like the Midwest and California. I felt Loveland had a present state of mind without much of a historical identity.

In addition, I did not find much ethnic or cultural diversity in Colorado. I used to joke with friends that, the "Welcome to Colorful Colorado" sign you see as you drive into the state must be in reference to geological formations, because it sure isn't a reflection of its people. Colorado, on the whole, is pretty much lily white.

As a child, if you had asked me to define my experiences with black people, I probably would have told you two things. I had a couple action figures of Lando Calrissian, the Billy Dee Williams character from the *Star Wars* trilogy, and I loved to moonwalk like Michael Jackson, which upon reflection was really more like a moonstagger.

One thing Colorado did have, though, was height. I still get giddy with excitement when I see the mountains for the first time as I fly into Denver International Airport or as I'm driving in my car west on I-70 from Kansas. The mountains call to me.

So my home state was culturally flat, but geologically incredible. I found Mississippi to be just the reverse.

* * *

The Mississippi Delta is the large alluvial flood plane of the Mississippi River, along the western border of Mississippi. This is more accurately the Yazoo-Mississippi Delta, springing from Greenville Mississippi to Memphis Tennessee. The Delta is a flat, 7,110 square mile swath of land, distinct both in geology and in culture. *(See map, p. xii)*

Except for the Choctaw Indians, the Delta was almost uninhabited by people up until the turn of the century.

Annual spring floods made sustainable living almost impossible, and the region remained a fertile, dense, jungle-like forest through the Civil War.

The dramatic transformation from dense forest to agricultural fields fascinated me. Once, while driving between Marks and nearby Clarksdale on Highway 6, I saw a small patch of forest amidst a vast cotton field. I stopped the car on the side of the road and walked into the woods. Although I was probably trespassing, I wanted to get a feel for what this land was like before becoming cultivated. I was engulfed by the trees the moment I walked in, and the brilliant sunshine was lost above the thick canopy, floored by dense undergrowth. It was a brief respite from much of the Delta I knew.

The fertile lands of the Delta were impossible to farm without large dikes to halt flooding from the Mississippi River, and the impassable forest needed to be cleared. At the end of 19th century, wealthy planters from around the South decided to take on the challenge, and sought to reap the financial rewards of the rich, dark soil. For this, they needed labor.

Slavery had halted 40 years prior, so the white wealthy planters' black labor alternative was sharecropping.

Recognizing their severely limited work opportunities, southern blacks moved to the Mississippi Delta in the thousands and began tilling the land. Many who initially came could still remember their days as slaves.

It took a few years and much arduous labor by many sharecropping blacks, but the dikes were erected along the river and much of the Delta's heavy forest was cleared. The Delta now stands as an eerily flat quilt of cotton fields, catfish farms, and other agricultural pastures crisscrossed with dusty roads, oases of dense forest, small towns, and the bright lights of casinos along the river.

* * *

Mississippi has a painful history of racism. Mississippi had more lynchings than any other state in the country, including the South. Slavery, sharecropping, Jim Crow, the White Citizens Council, and fear were a reality for blacks for well over a hundred years in Mississippi.

Before the public schools became integrated in the 1950's, the school system in the South was compulsory in its segregation. The axiom of "separate but equal" was a painful false tease to blacks in these states. In 1940, the average annual expenditure to a white public school student in the South was $40.39. A black student was a paltry $16.52, 41% of their white counterpart. In Mississippi, these numbers were even more extreme. While the average annual expenditure to a white public school student in Mississippi was lower at $31.33, the black student expenditure was only 22% of that figure at a mere $6.64. [1]

When future civil rights activist, Fannie Lou Hamer, was a child working on Delta plantations during the 1920s, she noticed although neither she nor her family had a working toilet, her boss's family pet had his own bathroom. "Negroes in Mississippi," Hamer concluded "are treated worse than dogs."[2]

Driving along Highway 61, between Cleveland and Clarksdale, one drives through the town of Mound Bayou. As you enter the city, a large billboard pronounces this a community started exclusively by former slaves.

On the outskirts of Clarksdale, 16 miles from Marks, blues singer Bessie Smith died following an automobile accident in 1937. <u>The white hospital refused to admit her bleeding black body, and she died while the search went out for a black ambulance.</u>[3] Ironically, a year before entering the Delta, I acted in a scene from "The Death of Bessie Smith" in a college play, holding the part of a surly doctor hitting on a nurse at the Clarksdale hospital. Focusing on all my speaking lines and developing the overall mood of my character, the story of the play took on a whole new meaning after making Mississippi my home.

Between Marks and Clarksdale sits an old black church and cemetery. I stopped a couple times to look at the gravesites. I saw old graves from the early and mid-twentieth century. These were the graves of hard, short lives and they left a haunting impression on me. I imagined tired, sweaty bodies coming home from a long day in the cotton field, enjoying a brief reprieve with one's self and family before sleep drifted one arduous day to the next.

And so the stories go.

The Delta has a unique history and subculture separate from the rest of the South, even the rest of Mississippi. The black population is 36 percent of the state—the highest in the country.[4] In the Mississippi Delta, the black population is more than double that.[5] The migrations for sharecropping jobs had much to do with that.

The hard labor required of the Delta also brought about incredible side products. Work hymns from the fields slowly evolved their way into the Delta Blues. Musical stories shared tales of onerous work, hard playing, and broken hearts.

When Robert Johnson was a boy, he was told he could not play the guitar—he simply did not have the gift of music. Johnson then went away to practice and perfect his

*Check on burial (white cemetry's in Michigan)

art for months by himself. When he returned, Johnson became the "Father of the Delta Blues." Due to this incredible reversal of talent, story has it that Robert Johnson sold his soul to the Devil late one night at the crossing of Highway 61 and Highway 49 in Clarksdale in order make him a world famous musician.

Today, a gas station sits adjacent to that intersection. Occasionally I filled my car there, and I noticed many tourists with out-of-state plates and Blues t-shirts visiting the famous crossing and taking pictures of each other at the monument placed at the intersection.

Only 33 when he died, Robert Johnson's death is shrouded in mystery. Whether by murder or natural causes, Johnson left only his short supply of recordings, two pictures of himself, and many broken hearts of the women he bedded.

I went through high school and college listening to musicians such as the Dave Matthews Band, Tracy Chapman, and Sting. However, when I discovered the multitudes of emotion and history within the lyrics of the Delta Blues, it joined my list of favorites.

Some parts of Delta history, chronicled by the blues, have ended—fire hoses used to control blacks, boycotts on segregated public facilities, lynches, murders of civil rights activists—but the growing pains of these momentous events have not.

The Civil Rights Movement has unfinished business in the Delta. The movement's victories for legal equality were all won by the early 1970s, but the emotional and economic segregation is still alive.

President Lyndon B. Johnson's "Great Society" welfare plan of the 1960's had quite an impact on the Delta, although there is no consensus on its success. Some believed Johnson's plan caused many blacks to become dependent on government assistance. One quote I heard frequently, by whites, in Mississippi was, "If you pay a black man on Thursday, you can guarantee he won't be in for work on Friday."

Others point to the second-class status of blacks in the South prior to the Johnson administration, and feel his legislation was an imperfect but necessary step forward when more independent opportunities were so feeble. Through Johnson's 1960s, the percentage of Mississippi blacks obtaining a high school diploma rose from 40 to 60 percent, and the enrollment of black voters jumped from 6 to 44 percent.[6] As some pointed out, if not welfare as the means to financial betterment for blacks in the Delta, then what was the better alternative toward equality? I found these two perspectives underscored much of the Delta psyche.

Before I moved to Mississippi, I saw poverty in purely economic terms. Poverty was simply an inability to buy adequate housing, a car, or proper food. In Quitman County, I realized that beyond this, poverty is an emotional state. Poverty is the recognition (whether believed or realized) that no matter how hard you work, your station in life prevents upward mobility. As a consequence of this, there is only the minimal motivation put forward to accomplish any of life's goals. It is the feeling that American vernacular like "There is no way to prosperity, prosperity is the way," "Just Do It" or "You Must Believe to Achieve" simply do not apply to you.

Seeking better opportunities following the mechanization of cotton, many blacks in the Delta moved to Northern cities. For some, real job opportunities did exist but that door was only open for a short time. Many blacks continued their struggles in cities like Chicago while others came back to the Delta.

Much of the Delta's white population started moving out around forty years ago, never to return. Many blacks with special skills also moved out of the Delta, once they recognized their talents could be better served in other parts of the country. A fellow teacher in Quitman County told me, "There just isn't anything for a college educated person to do in this town except teach." The "brain drain" left a huge hole—the vacancies of dilapidated business districts in many of these towns serve as testimony. Abandoned buildings looked strangled with kudzu, invasive vines that can grow over the outside walls of a house or a telephone pole almost overnight.

SAME APPLYS TODAY

While Colorado struggled to find itself an identity with its thin history, Mississippi glorified and suffocated in its own. With Confederate flags on front license plates, the heritage is still alive and well. At halftime during Ole Miss football games, in Oxford, forty-five miles east of Marks, plantation pillars are rolled out on the field and flag twirlers dance around them as the band plays "Dixie." And another reminder of times past: the socio-economic disparity between whites and blacks can still be drawn in places with a line as sharp as a railroad track.

As a white Colorado kid with no drawl, I did not know my official role in this tangled web of memoirs and neither of our backgrounds gave us much to go on. Mississippi was figuring me out, just as I did it.

CHAPTER 4

QC

Southern writer and University of Georgia history professor James C. Cobb once wrote he was "standing in a cotton field on the outskirts of Marks, Mississippi, describing the Mississippi Delta as a land of astounding economic and social disparity and declaring it 'the most southern place on earth.'"[7] When he wrote that, Dr. Cobb was standing a half-mile from my house.

Marks is the county seat of Quitman County—QC, for short. The county consists of nine small towns: Belen, Crenshaw, Crowder, Darling, Falcon, Lambert, Marks, Sledge, and Vance which occupy four hundred square miles. A third of the population lives below the poverty line and more than a quarter of QC has a disability.[8] The unemployment rate is 17.7 percent, ranking it 78th out of Mississippi's 82 counties.[9]

QC is classic rural living, but it is not culturally isolated. Marks sits about 40 miles east of the Mississippi

River and its casinos, 45 miles from the University of Mississippi (otherwise known as Ole Miss), and about sixty miles from Memphis. With a county population of a little more than ten thousand, Marks was the largest town, at 2,500, in the 2000 Census. Marks was also the only town with a traffic light—a red flashing stoplight that intersects the highway and Main Street.

Sometimes painful and other times inspiring, QC's history is an open stage of humanity. Blacks and whites alike struggled through the hot and humid weather, the arduous work of tilling the land, deep spiritual beliefs, and interracial life.

The first true settler was a trapper, woodsman, and planter named Thomas Hill. Hill brought more than 100 slaves with him into the county, looking to create a great plantation in the heart of the Delta. Fearing slave rebellions, panther, bear, and other wild animals from the dense forest, Hill had his plantation built within thick brick walls. This plantation building would become the first courthouse in the County. When Hill died, his slaves buried him in a Choctaw Indian ceremony along the Coldwater River.10

After Hill came, John A. Quitman, a Jewish Mississippi Congressman from New York, arrived, after whom QC was later named. Quitman only lived in his county for two years and died when poison was presumably secretly placed in his food during President Buchanan's inauguration in 1856.[11]

The next major figure with, ultimately, the longest impact, was a 20-year-old elected Sergeant at Arms from Bucksnort (now Independence), Mississippi named P. M. B. Self. Using the savings he acquired on his $4/ day salary, borrowing money, selling his horse and other possessions,

Self arrived in the Delta in 1904 to start a general county store in Marks, population 400. Self eventually had enough success to start buying farmland, which eventually amounted to thousands of acres. Self's quote, "Make the people around you prosperous and you will be prosperous yourself," was an epitaph for how he worked and lived. He was part classic Southern gentleman and part Renaissance man, eventually owning several cotton gins and an oil mill, and becoming President of the Citizen's Bank and Trust Company.[12]

Finally after several decades, Self's son, William King, returned home from the navy and World War II to take over the family business. This cemented the Self's long-standing family dynasty, galvanizing the county.

At the same time, blacks rarely held positions of power or prestige, and the Freedom Summer Project of 1964 had its share of casualties in Marks. In 1965, an election campaign worker was forced off the road, beaten, and urinated upon by four whites.[13] A year later, Martin Luther King, Jr. visited Marks as part of the Poor People's Movement and, "literally wept at the poverty of the black people there."[14] The two races were more neighbors by circumstance than camaraderie.

However, the county has produced some black success stories. Charley Pride, a country western singer, lived in Falcon and still owns an impressive house along Highway 3. A modern-day example is Val Towner who, with his talents in public policy and entrepreneurship, elected to stay in Marks. Towner was the principal of the middle school and owner of the popular restaurant The Dining Room by his late twenties, before winning the election for Quitman County School Board Superintendent. Towner stayed because his life was uncomplicated and his family lived in Marks. However, he wonders how long that will be enough. Towner said, "There are very few of us who stay and try to improve things. If things don't get better, there are going to be fewer of us."[15]

Today, the economy of Quitman County runs off what I call the "3 C's": cotton, catfish, and casinos. Cotton became king under the Self family but modern farming methods have made the old large labor force obsolete. Catfish then followed as a cash-worthy crop. Since 1990, casinos glow with light along the Mississippi River, employing Quitman County residents, to nearby Tunica and West Helena, northwest of Marks.

During my first week in Marks, I had to get my Mississippi drivers license in the County Courthouse. Upon walking out of the building, I noticed large letters carved in the white stone: "Obedience to the Law Sets You Free." The civil libertarian in me was enraged at such leash-and-collar advice. I was brought up to question authority and, then, to respect it if deserving. What would Martin Luther King, Jr. or Mahatma Gandhi say to such blind submission?

Then I took a step back, and I watched. In the hot, humid August sun, I saw men in white shirts and green striped pants cutting hedges, mowing lawns, and sweeping the streets. These men were not county employees; they were prisoners from the nearby jail at Parchman, thirty miles away. Perhaps the quote was not antithetical to human freedoms but a healthy reminder of simply how to behave. Although I was brought to Quitman County to teach, I found it was Quitman County that had the lessons to give.

CHAPTER 5

Reinventing Education

From kindergarten to my senior year of high school, I went through public school. After a childhood of Cub Scouts, trumpet lessons, student government, sports, and even ballet, I felt I was ready for college. It just seemed like the thing I was supposed to do.

Teaching in Marks, Mississippi completely changed a lot of my perceptions of public education. Even the things I believed I could take for granted were up for serious question. Even the articulation of my name became suspect.

On my first day of school, I noticed a recurrent pronunciation mishap. All of my players and students were calling me Coach Hoake (sounds like h"oak"). I tried to explain that my name had the same pronunciation as the classical music composer Bach, but with an "H." Unfortunately, it was becoming perfectly clear that neither my students nor football players listened to much Baroque, so Bach was not helping me. Finally by the third day of school, I had enough of Coach Hoake. I sketched a hawk on the chalkboard before my first period class. Underneath the drawing I wrote, "Coach Hach is Coach Hawk."

When my class started walking in a few minutes later, I told everyone we needed some clarification before we began class. I tapped on the chalkboard with my knuckles at the hawk drawing, and told everyone this is how you pronounce my name. An awkward silence descended on the class. Finally one of my students, Trenis, raised his hand and said, "Oh, you mean like a hoake, right Coach?" I gave up.

Understanding dialects was a real test for me. There were times that first year when I would have to ask students to repeat themselves, because I was unable to understand what they were saying. Usually after the third attempt, I was too embarrassed to say, "I'm sorry, could you repeat that again," so I just ended up smiling, nodding, and saying, "Yep, good point."

Moments like this typified my frequent ineptitude at communication in general. My worldview and theirs infrequently agreed. As much as I was utterly bewildered by their behavior, I knew they were equally confused by mine. For example, I could not figure out why so many of our students were having babies and then not showing parental concern, either financial or emotional. I would watch the growing bulge of pregnancy over a number of months, as the girls continued immature behavior including speaking out during class, fighting, and teasing fellow students. Then after a month off to deliver and care for their newborn, they were up to the same mischief. Wouldn't having a baby force one to grow up quickly? It was proven to me time and again in Mississippi, it did not. Usually, that mature parenting burden was placed on the grandparent's shoulders.

Likewise, my students could not understand how I got to be 24-years-old and not have either children or a wife. Many of my students decided I must be gay or, in their language, "a punk." As one of my students once told me, "Coach Hoake, if someone is in their mid-twenties and has no kids or a wife, then something is wrong. You just gotta be a punk."

All the time, I had to shed my Colorado value system, or I was not going to get anywhere. The racial demographics had certainly reversed themselves. As a student, Loveland High School was 92 percent white.[16] As a teacher, MS Palmer High School was 2 percent white.[17]

Education was essentially defined the same in the Delta and Colorado, but this definition manifested itself in different ways. First of all, the schools were segregated. Sure, Brown vs. Board of Education slammed its gavel on the integration of public schools fifty years prior, but the schools were still segregated. When public school integration legislation made its way to the Delta in the 1960s, the white community simply erected all-white private academies. In Marks, the Delta Academy was established with the Rebel Raider mascot, a confederate soldier on a horse waving a confederate flag. Although the rest of Mississippi finally allowed integration to unfold in the school system, the Delta largely continued to segregate legally through academies.

In the hallways of M.S. Palmer High School, beside the basketball gym, stood a testimony to the school's history.

The senior class of each year was framed from the 1940s through the present day. A complete history of innocent, smiling 18-year-olds, covering decades of legal and cultural change, can be viewed in those hallways. Many of the earlier pictures had faded and were covered in dust, but the story within the pictures still stands.

The pre-integration pictures of the 1940s and 1950s displayed only black students at what was then the Marks Agricultural High School. The white public high school class pictures were not included on the walls. Then in the 1960s, the pictures show an infusion of white faces. This continues for a few years, and then through the 1970s, the white faces diminish again as white students were pulled from the public schools and put into the academies or left the Delta all together. I found something haunting about the rise and fall of integration in Quitman County, like riding the crest of a wave and then feeling it slowly die under your feet.

Secondly, I found a level of apathy I had never seen before. When I was a student, there were always the overachievers and the slackers, but never have I seen an entire academic culture breed apathy. The majority of the students had little concern for their successes or failures, and what little interest was generated typically revolved around grades, not the pursuit of knowledge. Even the faculty seemed indifferent. I would walk through the halls and see classrooms with students with their heads down on their desks, teachers passing time, and videos unrelated to schoolwork glaring on a television screen.

If quality teachers were hard to come by, quality substitute teachers were even rarer. During my second year of teaching, I saw occasional substitutes who were seniors at the school the year before. They would look at me and say, "Hey Coach Hoake, I'm just subbing in today."

Of course there were exceptions—Mr. Dean enthusiastically taught three social studies subjects and coached four sports; Ms. Hughes spent her life teaching English at the school; and Mr. Pryor taught chemistry, started a community little league baseball association, coached softball, and led the Sunday choir at his local church—but that's what they were, exceptions.

Parental apathy was also a problem. During one occasion of a school-wide parent teacher conference, it looked really ugly. No report cards were given out that night, so there was no transcript incentive to bring parents into the school. Instead, this was an opportunity for parents and teachers to discuss their children's strengths and weaknesses and talk about ways to make progress. I sat behind my desk for three hours and no parent came to my door. I did a little lesson planning, read a book, and joked around with a few fellow teachers to pass the time. As it turned out, only seven parents showed up that night.

For students, the very culture was keeping some of the brightest back from showing their intelligence. It was not hip for students to focus on their studies and work hard. There was constant peer pressure to give into complacency and show the minimum productivity possible. However, there was a small movement within the student body to overcome this apathy. Students, who courageously motivated themselves for self-improvement, called those who were trying to submerge them "haters." Hardworking students said they had to "shake dem haters off." Figuratively, students would brush air off their shoulders free of "haters," symbolizing that they could not be undeterred from having a strong work ethic. At pep assemblies, the student body would chant "shake dem haters off! shake dem haters off!" in a rhythmic, rap-like procession.

My first day as a teacher was supposed to be August 10, 1998. The night before school started, the administration decided the school district was not ready for the new school year and postponed it for a week.

When it finally began, the first weeks were a nightmare. School starts mid-August but about 25 percent of the students don't show up until after Labor Day because they are completing their summer vacation away from Mississippi in places like Chicago. I wasn't sure if I was to get started with my lessons and assignments and have the 25 percent catch up when they arrived, or keep things slow until after Labor Day.

I had thirteen textbooks in my classroom for my students to share—there were 62 students in my six classes. I asked a veteran teacher at the school what she would recommended I do with regard to homework and so few books since there not enough for each of my students to take home each night. The teacher looked at me curiously, like I had asked the question in some foreign alien language. After a long pause, she said, "Oh, they don't do homework here."

Most students disliked doing much work. They frequently criticized me for pushing them too hard. "Coach Hoake, you know this just ain't right. What are you, some kind of slave driver?" Sometimes, students would get so livid they'd slam their books on the desk, stand up, and call me a bully.

To say that I was the shining beacon at the school is a lie. There were days I'd get lazy and play a video related to my class work, and even this tactic didn't go as planned. I once had my classes watch the film, *The Long Walk Home*, starring Sissy Spacek and Whoopi Goldberg, about the bus boycott in Montgomery Alabama following Rosa Parks' decision to not leave her seat at the front of the bus. At one point in the film, two white teenage boys are chasing a black teenage girl through a city park. The boys push the girl down and call her names. As the violence escalated, many of my students got caught up in the thrill of the cruelty and cheered support for the boys. As the only white person in the classroom, I was shocked.

Fortunately, there were also positive things to cheer about. Pep rallies were a regular Friday afternoon event. I enjoyed the rallies and sometimes got behind the microphone to give a brief motivational speech and yell to the various classes, "We have spirit, yes we do! We have spirit, how about you?" The class that yelled the loudest received the M.S. Palmer Spirit Stick. It seemed to really get the kids in a frenzy of enthusiasm. Once, a student came up to me and said I did a great job, but that I said it wrong. He told me it was, "We got spirit," not "We have spirit." I told him I appreciated him telling me the error of my grammatical ways. I laughed out loud, and cried inside.

I also spent my mornings in the school gym—two out of every six weeks meant morning duty. As the students came in off their buses, they each had a small breakfast from the cafeteria and then sat in the gym bleachers until the morning bell rang. During morning duty, another teacher and I would stand in the gym facing all the students, watching carefully in case a fight broke. It felt like being an early morning bouncer in a night club.

On one occasion, one of my students, Derrick, got himself into a fist fight with a girl. Derrick was a pretty small fellow and was not fairing well. In fact, he was getting pummeled. The moment I saw this, I jumped into the crowded bleachers to break it up. As I was separating Derrick and the girl, she lashed out one last swing. It missed Derrick but hit me right in the temple. Within a few seconds, both Derrick and the girl were on their way to the assistant principal's office. However, after the bell rang and as I walked to my classroom, a number of students looked at me and said, "Hey, Coach Hoake, that sure is one fine shiner you got on this mornin.'"

Theft, too, was a common occurrence. Small items like pencils and candy were stolen almost regularly. I had a pair of sunglasses taken and I did not have a clue who'd stolen them, just that they were gone at the end of the day. I told each of my classes that the sunglasses had been a gift from my sister and I desperately wanted them back. To my surprise, the glasses sat on my desk the next morning. On another occasion, a substitute teacher stole a video of Disney's *Tarzan* from my desk. That item, I never had returned.

Another surprise was the paddle. When I was an elementary school student, I heard a rumor the principal had paddled a misbehaving student. I was frightened of this story, even if it was fictional. In the Delta, the paddle was real. Corporal punishment was a way of life.

Our assistant principal, Mr. Keys, was the man in charge of school discipline. Mr. Keys had the famous football coach Bear Bryant's approach to discipline—very stern but fair. Keys had a difficult job and although he did not personally like corporal punishment, it was what he was familiar with. More importantly, it was what the student body recognized as stern discipline.

Some students were paddled almost daily. Sometimes, I would see a standing single file of students coming out of the office, waiting to be paddled. After a paddling I saw students walking gingerly back to class with one hand holding a hall pass from the principal's office and their other hand gently holding their bottom.

For myself, I could never imagine paddling a student. I have always felt violence is the absolute last resort to solving a conflict. Not in the Delta.

Although I never personally paddled a student, I did send misbehaving students down to Mr. Keys's office. I am not proud of this fact, but I saw it as a practical necessary evil. I recognized how difficult behavior management was without paddling. I could not allow my principles of nonviolence to supersede a misbehaving student's potential to completely undermine my authority and prevent other students from learning. That said, I do not know if I did the wrong thing by sending students to get paddled, or if I should have thought harder to find other means of discipline. In fact, the first time I finally gave in and wrote up a hall pass to the principal's office for an unruly student to get paddled, the other students clapped and cheered me on, saying I was "finally teaching some control." My circumstances mixed with my limited time and imagination allowed corporal punishment into my life for two years.

Finally, there were the details.

M.S. Palmer High School did not have lockers. It was felt there would be too much theft if lockers went up and down the hallways. Instead, students carried all their belongings with them wherever they went.

Also, there was no uniform ceiling. It was a collection of rafters holding an upper ceiling above it. Occasionally mice would use the rafters as walkways across the class-room, walking gingerly over the heads of my students. Also, the ceiling did not always prevent rain from entering. Many times, puddles of water accumulated on the floor after a big rainstorm. The desks were arranged to avoid the wet spots. The rain warped and bubbled my chalkboard as well as ruined a motivational poster I had handmade with Crayola markers using the line from former Notre Dame's football coach Lou Holtz, "Attitude Is Everything," making it all but illegible.

Plumbing was also a problem. The useable toilets changed often over the course of the year. I would jump from the teacher's lounge to the student restroom and back again. Even toilet paper was in short supply. I frequently brought my own, and let my students use it as needed. Below is a hallway announcement stating the plumbing problem in the school, and that we were not to use tissue for the toilets. I am not sure what was more appalling, the status of the plumbing, the patriotism, or the misspelling of the word "toilet." *(See page 38.)*

Structurally, culturally, even behaviorally, I found my-self divorcing my educational standards and adopting new ones. Only four years prior I was a high school student myself. Before I left for Mississippi, I questioned if I had grown enough to make that leap. Little did I know the biggest leap would be reinventing public education alto-gether.

CHAPTER 6

Rambo

The principal of M.S. Palmer was Rambo. That wasn't his real name but everyone called him Rambo and that's how he liked it. In fact, he had "RAMBO" inscribed into his leather belt. He was a powerful, muscular man who drove a towering monster truck into school everyday and wore steel-tipped cowboy boots. His personality matched his Rambo visage even better than his appearance ... not quite the principal model I was accustomed to.

I heard many horror stories about M.S. Palmer High School, pre-Rambo. I heard stories of students running amok both in the school and around the streets of Marks. A friend told me he had to swerve his truck once off the road in front of the school in order not to hit the many students running out of the building. Students left lunch trays littering the cafeteria.

Then, in 1997, Rambo arrived.

With Principal Rambo's iron-fist approach to discipline, the school took a dramatic turn. Classrooms became quieter, fights lessened, and test scores rose. Out of the gate, Rambo's control worked. From the variety of meals served in the cafeteria, to the bus schedule, to the success of the sports teams—Rambo had his hand in everything.

The local police force was no longer needed to frequent the school. Many felt, particularly within the white community, who had less invested in the black school, the police were neglecting many parts of the county because they were so busy at the high school. Strong-willed Rambo was the cure.

However, life under Rambo's strict regimen was not wholly peaceful either.

Principal Rambo served in the military with combat duty in Vietnam. When he walked through the halls with his intense eyes, there were times I felt he was not so much looking for mischief from students so much as still looking for Vietcong.

Rambo's discipline was mixed with a kind of egalitarianism. He might requisition a teacher with years of teaching experience out of a classroom before school to start folding napkins for him for a lunch meeting later in the day. Many feared him, hoping to avoid him whenever possible. The threat of receiving a good chewing out was directly related to your proximity to Rambo.

Rambo believed teachers held almost all the responsibility for students' success or failure and constantly demanded that we hold ourselves and our students to higher standards of obedience and improvement. Once in a faculty meeting, he admitted, "Okay, these aren't the easiest students in the world to teach. But like a football coach can only coach the players he's got, we can only teach the students we've got. We can't import talent or determination." On another occasion, he told the faculty "Do you know who the greatest Civil War general was? Many think it was Robert E. Lee, but it wasn't. The greatest Civil War general was the true innovator Nathan Bedford Forrest, whose resourcefulness started guerilla war tactics that the Union could not respond to. We need that same kind of innovation in our classrooms." I always thought that was an odd example for innovative teaching—Nathan Bedford Forrest was also the founder of the Ku Klux Klan.

The emotional distance between Rambo's serenity and fuming anger were only a half-breath from each other. Rambo had no qualms about commenting on teachers' discipline methods in front of their students. He also made on the spot administrative decisions that had dramatic ripple effects within the school.

Occasionally, Principal Rambo would hold impromptu assemblies with all of the students in the gym at the start the school day, with the intent to motivate. These were unique events where he would expound on his views on the school and on life; whatever the subject, he had an opinion:

Behavior

"Sometimes," he would say, "I watch the misbehavior in this school (shaking his head), and I just wonder what Martin Luther King would say about the way these young black Americans are acting."

Communication
"Don't talk about people, talk to people."

Religion
"We all know it all comes back to Jesus Christ."

Faculty Obedience
"Never question or show disrespect to the person who signs your paycheck."

Leadership
"What's up with all these girls in student leadership? We need the boys to step up and show where real leadership comes from."

Work ethic
"You can't make chicken salad out of chicken shit."

Principal Rambo kept the school in control, mostly out of fear of his larger-than-life presence. Students were afraid; but, all agreed that classrooms had became quieter, fights had lessened, and test scores had risen under his regime.

As a teacher, I had a few run-ins with Principal Rambo.

My most memorable moment with Rambo happened during the sports banquet at the end of my second year of teaching. I was at the podium talking about the football season and presenting individual awards. One of the key players, Kraven, who was receiving an award for great defensive play, was unable to attend the banquet. When all the trophies were handed out, Rambo came up behind me at the podium whispered to me to quickly to make up an award to give to Troy—one of my special needs students and a hardworking, selfless senior defensive end and full-back. Troy was the only one at his table who had not received an award. He sat there with his arms crossed, looking up at the ceiling, dressed in a pressed shirt and tie. Rambo pulled the name "Kraven" off the remaining trophy and handed it too me, whispering, "I'll buy Kraven a new one and give it to him next week." I then turned back to the audience and declared Troy "Mr. Football for the 1999 season." Troy was elated and gave me a hug as he received his trophy. As I left the stage, I turned to Rambo and told him that was a wonderful thing he had just done. He just smiled back in response.

[handwritten margin note: TROPHY TO AN DISABLE STUDENT by Rambo]

My personal feelings for Rambo ran between distaste, admiration, and fear. As Rambo used to say, "You may love me or you may hate me but you will always remember me." Although I never felt I understood him, I sensed he was trying to do what he felt was right the vast majority of the time.

On one of my last days at the school, I was walking across an empty basketball gym, heading toward my classroom. Principal Rambo stopped me to say I was one of the finest people in education he had ever known and, without waiting to see my reaction, he walked on. I stood in the quiet gym, speechless.

PLEASE DON'T PUT
TISSUE IN THE TOLIET

Tissue warning from the hallway of M. S. Palmer High School.

CHAPTER 7

Sped (Special Education)

I can remember being in first grade when we were first assigned reading groups. Each group had a color and depending on our strengths as readers, we were grouped with other students of similar ability. I was in the green group: average. Even at age six, I could see a hierarchy developing around me.

Similarly, every high school student knows where he or she stands in the academic hierarchy. There are grade point averages, standardized tests, class ranks, and other quantifying devices that clearly show your station on the scholastic measuring stick.

At M.S. Palmer, I was a special education social studies teacher. I soon realized that no student understands where he or she stands in pecking order on the scholastic measuring stick better than the special education student.

Two weeks before my first school year started, a fellow special education teacher told me I shouldn't focus so much on reading or writing skills but should spend time on basic life skills. She gave me a large binder filled with life skills lesson plans, published specifically for the special education teacher. One lesson plan included a sheet of paper with various pictures of tools—a shovel, a lawnmower, and a rake. The students were supposed to name which tool was which.

I thought to myself, these are high school kids, some of whom are on my football team. Surely, my classes are going to be above this. Aren't they? One my fellow football coaches told me "You don't want to teach special ed. for too long or you will end up as crazy as they are."

As it turns out, a "special education" student in Mississippi could mean any number of things: a victim of fetal alcohol syndrome, a former crack baby, a neglected child with behavioral problems, an academically slower student with very caring parents or a student with a criminal record. There were poignant cases of students who had been put into special education early in their elementary school careers to take advantage of greater welfare assistance for families of special education children. By the time these students reached high school, they were sometimes too far behind to be placed in classes with their peers.

Although the class was made up of so many types of students, one quality many shared was the longing for a voice that really, genuinely mattered in the world.

I had no idea what skills my students were going to have, or how best to teach them. Should I teach American history like a social studies teacher, as it stated on my job description? Should I teach life skills such as "what does a pitchfork look like?" Should I teach something different all together?

As a social studies teacher, I really wanted my students to learn how to read. I decided to use social studies material to improve literacy. The United States history textbooks I was given were written at the fifth grade level.

During the first week I found a four-paragraph story in my fifth grade level American history book about Orson Wells' radio scare of the "War of the Worlds" from 1938. The story discusses the details surrounding Orson Wells' fictional radio newscast about aliens attacking earth. At the time the radio show aired, many of the listeners believed the story to be true and panicked accordingly. The story looked intriguing enough to provoke student interest, so I typed the story into my computer and made it into a pre-test.

The students were to read the four-paragraph story as many times as they wanted, and then return it when they felt they understood the material. I then gave them four comprehension questions about the content of the story. All of my students, in all six classes, took this test. My results came back as follows:

$$
\begin{array}{rcl}
A &=& 0 \\
B &=& 0 \\
C &=& 3 \\
D &=& 6 \\
F &=& 26
\end{array}
$$

Some students made up answers. Some wrote things like, "I don't no, Coch!" Some wrote nothing and handed back the blank piece of paper, saying it was a stupid test. Some wrote a portion of a sentence from the story, as well as they could remember, that displayed the same words from the question.

After that experiment, I elected to teach from the book, but only the last hundred years of US history—the material I felt most relevant to their lives. I would start with the Spanish - American War in 1898 and move forward to the present day. By cutting my curriculum by almost two-thirds, I could spend more time focusing on students' individual reading skills. To compensate for the fact I did not have enough books for all the students, I copied each day's section from the book and made mini-packets for each student to work from.

My first week was spent on the three-month Spanish-American war. We slowly went over the challenging words, discussed where the battles took place, what war was, how the key personalities played into the conflict, and what impact the media had in the way the country perceived the war.

At the end of the seventh hour on Friday, I thought I needed to throw a few questions out to check comprehension of my first real week of teaching. I selected one of my more academically challenged students, Cheri, and asked, "Cheri, who won the Spanish-American War?"

She looked at me through her thick rimmed glasses, which she desperately needed but infrequently wore because she felt they took away from her attractiveness to the boys.

After a long pause, Cheri said tentatively, "Asia?"

Thirty seconds later the bell rang and my students were excitedly walking down the hall toward the buses to take them home for the weekend. I sat at my desk with my head in my hands, on the verge of tears. I felt like the worst teacher in the world—like Teach For America for me was more like Seriously Wasting Everyone's Time For America.

* * *

As time went on, I slowly learned how to work with each student, depending on their academic, social, and emotional needs. I recognized I could really damage a student's confidence by putting them on the spot in a place of academic weakness. I felt bad about how I'd handled Cheri and was determined to be more aware in such situations.

Still, there were moments that surprised me.

Every class started with a journal entry, sparked by a question on the chalkboard. One day I wrote, "Which country in the world do you believe has the greatest number of people?" A student in my second period class, Cory, responded with, "I think it's Jackson, Mississippi because that is where the White House is." It was beyond anything I was prepared for.

Another hurdle was humiliation. The special education students were mercilessly made fun of by some in the mainstream student majority. Regular students would walk by my room during class and say, "Hey, Coach Hoake, give my best to your speds, okay?" I looked at my students sitting at their desks, after hearing this derogatory acronym for special education students, and I could visualize their fragile self-esteems quietly being chiseled away.

Many of the high school students felt that I, too, had once been a special education student, accounting for the fact I was now a special education teacher. I would sit in non special education classes as a substitute teacher occasionally during my planning period when a teacher was sick. Sometimes the students would tell me, "Coach, you seem smart enough to teach regular ed. students." I shrugged off this logic and responded by saying that "we are all special in different ways."

My students were not ostracized solely by other students, but sometimes by the other high school teachers as well. During my second year of teaching, one of the high school teacher's students put together a science fair in the gym, open for all students to come observe. When my students walked into the gym to look at the exhibits, the teacher told me very loudly, "I don't want your special students getting too close to our exhibits. They'll all be up to no good." I was appalled and told her that my students would be just fine.

The worst treatment, however, came from within the classroom by fellow special education students. If a student was struggling to read something out loud in class, a fellow classmate would speak out, "You're such a sped," and shake his or her head.

Recognizing their lowered positions on the scholastic totem pole, they were constantly competing to not end up dead last. My students could be ruthless to each other, releasing their insecurities back and forth in grudge matches. It broke my heart and I constantly tried to curb that behavior. A recurrent theme I repeatedly said was, "Don't compete to be better than other students but compete to be better than you used to be."

＊ ＊ ＊

To reach my students, I figured out what their interests were and then mapped out analogies and reading exercises that matched. My students read about the rap star "Masta P," professional wrestling, and popular movies along with social studies. I took my limited imagination as far as I could. However, looking back, I could have done far more.

My second year of teaching, I taught high school special education science. Instead of working with a textbook,

I wrote a text that was as user friendly and interesting as I could come up with, frequently including student names, jokes, and classroom trivia. I made enough copies for each of my students, as well as enough extras for students who lost one, for a reduced grade.

This system worked much better and gave me more room to focus on individual needs. My lessons were far from perfect and there were certainly moments of lag time, but overall there was marked improvement.

Progress was difficult, however, as approximately 25 percent of my students were absent on any given day. Apathy vastly outnumbered illness, family commitments, or giving birth (for my student mothers) as the greatest cause for nonattendance, regardless of the wide range of excuses given to me.

Some students would miss weeks on end. There were a few times every student in my class was absent, and I sat in my classroom alone. I grew up thinking school was something you simply needed to attend, but many of my students took a distinctly different approach.

Each day, Rambo made a list of absentees based on homeroom roll calls. This list was exhaustingly long and proportionally longer still among the special education students. Along with other teachers, I tried to create an environment where the student really felt wanted and needed as a daily part of the class. However, the competition of television and other non-school attractions frequently proved too much to overcome.

Okay, so you are a black special education student in the Mississippi Delta. You are sixteen or seventeen and currently reading at the second-grade level. Your parents' investment in your education is moderate to non-existent.

You may have a child or two of your own and a criminal record. You have a white teacher fresh from college who is basically a kid himself, from some place hundreds of miles away attempting to motivate you to learn. You recognize that if you give in to the teacher's enthusiasm, there is an outside chance your reading skills could increase as much as a grade level over the course of the year. Say you do this and it is a year later, and you are now seventeen or eighteen. What have you accomplished? You would now be reading at the third-grade level. In life, in your career options, in your ability to interact or not interact with the world, how much improvement was the sacrifice worth?

This was the conundrum I privately asked myself during those few seconds between franticly running off copies, completing lesson plans, and grading papers.

Despite all this, there were many students who really did try and worked very hard. There were also parents who cared. I had students like Stephanie and Nikita who I feel were among the hardest working, disciplined, and noble students anywhere in the country, whether it be in an M.S. Palmer High School special education classroom or a PhD seminar at Harvard University.

My students, with their shortcomings, insecurities, and immaturity, were among the most genuine people I have ever met. Although I probably taught them a few things about history, reading, and science, I know they taught me far more. They taught me how to reach out to someone, how to be firm, how to not rush to judgment, how to be patient, and how to find joy in any circumstance.

CHAPTER 8

Tales on and Beyond the Gridiron

Soon after first being introduced to the game on the recess playing fields of Monroe Elementary School, I played my first season of organized tackle football with the Loveland Midget Athletic Association in 1987 as a scrawny sixth grade tight end. From there I continued playing through high school as an option quarterback, and eventually as a defensive back and kick returner in college. I loved the game of football—from the emotional intensity to the team atmosphere to the autumnal changing of the seasons.

The beauty of the game is found when all the time spent in the weight room, watching game film, practicing, and understanding your strategy, coalesce on game day. Only after the conclusion of much hard work can you divorce yourself from thinking through every play, formation, and scheme and react on instinct, allowing your emotions to take over. To me, football was nothing more than a game of preparation, both mental and physical. I found if that if there is any virtue to victory it is that it is most frequently bestowed on the team that has most properly prepared; thus, a reasonable analogy for life.

However, when I became a football coach for the M.S. Palmer Dragons, I found no amount of preparation could have equipped me for what I was about to experience.

Just seconds after my opening teaching interview with Principal Rambo, I was approached by the new head football coach, athletic director, and world history teacher Aaron Holden, who asked me to be the defensive back's coach. This was Holden's first year at the school, and he was still putting his coaching staff together. However, I was uncertain if I would have the time to do it well. I joined Teach For America to teach and had no intention to coach. But because I played that position in college I decided to accept the job.

I discovered coaching involved a great deal more than strategic X's and O's. Putting together a successful football program in Marks, Mississippi required a great, great deal more than that. A football coach had to clean the field house (a locker room/ weight room), help sod the field (which included the occasional attacks of fire ants), and drive players home across the county after practice (which we eventually did in our own cars). I became part of a collection of rookie coaches that Aaron Holden took under his wing. Holden made a point to mentor both coaches and players alike.

The Dragons had fielded few wins in years past—the team was 1-9 the year before. In fact, Coach Holden was so disgusted by the level of play he saw, he had us cut the first practice short to talk to the coaches alone. As we shuffled into a tiny dilapidated, unventilated coach's office, Holden told us with a deeply frustrated tone, "We had ourselves a junior high team out there. That was just awful, plain and simple. Men, we clearly have our work cut out for ourselves." Holden had been the linemen's coach from the nearby town of Clarksdale, which had won a state championship the season before, raising his already lofty expectations for what was deemed acceptable.

Players, too, held exceedingly high hopes for gridiron glory, even if they were unjustified. Tiny was a junior, a father of a little girl, and a second string linebacker. However, this did not deter him from telling the coaching staff he intended to play at the University of Michigan. Tiny said he had watched a Michigan game on television and was impressed enough at what he saw to become a member on the team upon graduating from M.S. Palmer. Later that evening, I sarcastically asked Coach Holden if Lloyd Carr (the head coach at Michigan) had been notified of Tiny's decision. With a quiet chuckle and shaking his head, Holden simply said, "Hell no."

This was football at both its most basic and complex level.

With a limited athletic budget, the players frequently wore different types of jerseys. We had a training room, but it appeared to have been abandoned a long time ago, now harboring far more cockroaches and mice than rolls of athletic tape. The locker room did not have a single working toilet or shower head. There was no toilet paper and many of the cleaning supplies that did exist were the ones I had purchased myself and brought in. Between the smell of the sweaty football pads, dirt, decay, and toilets that continued to be used long after their flushing days had expired, along with the accumulated stench of body odor, it left a dizzying effect for the uninitiated who ventured into the locker room. Even our rickety stadium appeared on its last leg. The old wooden bleacher stands wobbled back and forth as you walked or sat on them. Some wooden planks were so weak it was advised to avoid them all together for fear of falling through.

When our new coaching staff first arrived, the football field in the stadium looked like a nature reserve, plush with a growing variety of weeds and wild onions. Our coaching staff put in long nights painting the lines on the field and clearing out the non-grass flora to make it playable. When the school mower broke down during the week leading into the Homecoming game, we each pitched in to pay for a local professional mower to make the field presentable.

Post-game review was not any easier as every Monday, I unplugged my television from my living room, and put it in the back seat of my car. Then, between after school bus duty and before practice, I brought the television into the field house so the team could critique their game from the Friday before. After evaluating the game, I carried my television back to my car and locked it in my car so it would not get stolen during the rest of practice.

As financial recognition for the three hours we spent every night through the three-month football season, each of our coaches received around $400 as a yearly stipend that was put into our teaching paycheck. Over the course of the school year, we each spent more money than that on gasoline alone, driving players home each night in our cars.

Throughout the year, we would play schools with varying levels of athletic budget funding. Some schools were almost as under-resourced as we were. Other schools had beautiful uniforms, a fully-furnished band, television monitors on the sidelines for coaches to check plays and schemes on the field, elaborate headset systems and an exhaustingly manicured playing field. We also played schools of widely dispersed racial dynamics. Some teams were predominantly white and others were almost entirely black, like us. There were a couple of games where I was the only white person on the field, among the coaches, players, media, and referees alike.

Our band may have lacked essential instruments, but we more than made up for this in dancing and bravado. Our cheerleaders and pom pom girls would swerve their hips and move in ways that always awakened the interest of M.S. Palmer supporters, even if it had nothing to do with our football team.

Our football program received unsurpassed support from two men in the community. Tyrone, our head team manager, showed up for almost every practice with enthusiasm and gracious manners. I knew nothing about Tyrone's past, except that he had had major head surgery during his younger years as proven by a few long scars along his head. The surgery had left Tyrone mentally slower and unable to use his left arm. However, he could still throw a 50 yard spiral bulls-eye with his right arm. Tyrone also offered the same support to the basketball team in the winter. No one supported M.S. Palmer sports with greater diligence and concern than Tyrone.

The other man, Boots, was also mentally slower and could hardly speak. Boots was always there for a handshake and a smile, and would volunteer to clean the locker room following every game. I virtually never heard a word uttered from Boot's lips nor even knew what his real name was, but he was always there and could always be counted on.

I thought I was way over my head for the first few weeks. I was overwhelmed by the combination of pre-season practices and not really knowing what I was doing in my classroom. I had even given more than token thoughts to quitting coaching. I felt it better to be proficient at one job than mediocre, at best, at two.

However, this sacrifice did payoff in the end. Many of our players were incredible athletes. The talent was raw, but when put together properly, was mesmerizing. When focused and attentive, I saw skills of execution I could not have imagined when I drew the plays up in the playbook.

During our first game, we played in Clarksdale against Coahoma-Aggie High School. Storming back from a large first half deficit, we took the lead in the fourth quarter, aided when our safety, Ray-J, intercepted a pass and returned it 30 yards for a touchdown. The victory felt euphoric and reminded me of what I loved about football, a love that had been forgotten in the smells, heat, and fatigue of August.

Later that evening as we returned to school on the bus, many members of the community honked their cars, waved their hands, whistled, and cheered their victorious team home. I began to recognize the importance of my second job.

Our second game took us to Grenada High School. This bigger school made us feel small, and we were beaten handily. Adding to the insult, we got lost on the way home. I remember looking out the window and seeing a street sign that said, "Entering Grenada County." As one coach in the car aptly put it, "Uh-oh, that doesn't look good." We arrived in Marks at 2:30 am on Saturday morning.

✸ During a road win at Drew High School (the alma-mater of ex-NFL quarterback Archie Manning) later that season, the police gathered our coaching staff to tell us that death threats had been placed against our team as our victory started to look imminent. The police told the players to put their pads and helmets back on, and they would escort us out of town in a route passing as few houses as possible. As I drove my Volkswagen in back of the players' bus, we were surrounded by cop cars and flickering lights. One of the coaches looked out my car window to the local onlookers yelling at us and said, quite matter of factly, that he would "carry a hand gun with him to each and every game from here on out." He did. ✸

The games were something to behold. I watched Coach Holden gather the players around him and silently let anticipation build. Then he would open the flood gates into a fiery oration where he would lift his players' emotions to a zenith pitch before releasing them onto the field. I watched the stadium lights swell with flying insects as they orbited the luminescence, or the herds of hundreds of black crickets that crept across the field to avoid being crushed by the game. I felt the emotional wave in the stadium between the moments of silence in the pre-game prayer to the end of the National Anthem applause.

The first season in 1998 ebbed and flowed to a 5-5 finish. Clearly this was not state-championship material, but looking at where we had come from, I felt this was a major step in the right direction. Many of the players were angered that we demanded so much from them during that first season. Clearly the players were unaccustomed to the stress and strain of focused strategy and physical sacrifice that were the pre-requisites for success. Some of the players rebelled and verbally chastised our coaching staff. One of our star linemen told our defensive coordinator to "Fuck off" when he attempted to keep order on a bus before driving away to a road game. The player was kicked off the team on the spot.

Slowly, however, the players began to realize we had their best interests in mind. As wins began to trickle in, our ability to reach our players continued to grow. Coach Holden made it a high priority to get his players college recruiting letters from such places as Coahoma Community College to the University of Alabama, motivating them to look past high school and see the potential value of football.

Although most of our athletes were not academically prepared for four year institutions right out of high school, football did provide scholarships to junior colleges. For many of our players, this was the only ticket to an education beyond high school.

During the winter that followed that first season, I was promoted to Offensive Coordinator. I purchased a few coaching videos on offensive philosophy, and rethought what I remembered from my own high school quarterbacking days. Over the course of a couple of weekends, I put together a fifty-six page offensive playbook.

During my second season in 1999, I was calling the offensive plays and we started slowly as the players adapted to the new offense. Mistakes were common place. The linemen missed blocking schemes. Our skill players forgot to go in motion. Our quarterback failed to run out his fakes.

After one early season game, Principal Rambo yelled at our coaching staff for being undisciplined. However, as the season continued, our execution became smoother and smoother.

In the second to last game, we played Water Valley, a high school from the hills outside the Delta. The towns in Mississippi outside the Delta had much smaller black/white racial demographics and usually, not surprisingly, more money. The solid favorite, Water Valley was a proven team with a far larger athletic budget. On this late October evening, we were locked in a tense game as the lead continued to flip-flop. As the forth quarter began to wind down and we were a few points behind, I called our quarterback to set up the option we had been executing over and over throughout the night. However, instead of running down the line through the same progression, quarterback Judge Collins dropped way back and flicked a screen pass to our running back, Andrew Dukes. In the foreign language of football lingo, our playbook titled the play, "Veer Right Dive Option Right Screen Comeback." Collins pinned the pass on Dukes' jersey, who then made a vicious cut and streaked alone down the sideline for the winning touchdown. A couple of minutes later, a couple players trounced me with water from a large orange Gatorade tub. It was one of my most fulfilling moments in Mississippi, not because of the touchdown or even the game, but because of all the work that lead up to that single moment.

The following week, we finished the regular season on the road with an 18-0 win over Charleston, a town about 30 miles southeast of Marks. We won our last three games and finished 6-4.

With all the excitement of surrounding the first win-

ning record in many years, no one knew the football program was about to hit an insurmountable wall.

Coach Aaron Holden had overcome incredible obstacles
in the short time I had known him. The summer I arrived,
Holden's son had died in a car accident. He usually never
mentioned it, but it was clearly tearing him up inside,
underneath his austere pretense. Then during late autumn
of my second year, Coach Holden's wife, Ruth, was diag-
nosed with breast cancer. Ruth went through an exhaust-
ing chemotherapy process, but, amazingly, he still held
his emotional ground.

Despite all his spent emotions, coupled with working
as a world history teacher and serving as the athletic director and head football coach, Holden was still voted as
the "Teacher of the Year" among students across the campus. He augmented academic learning with messages and
anecdotes on how to live life that the student body readily
understood. The students simply adored him.

Then in late January 2000, Coach Holden had a signifi-
cant stroke that paralyzed the left side of his body. As a
coaching staff, we did not know what to do. We went to
lunch at a local restaurant and quietly told each other
that it looked like football at M.S. Palmer would go with
him. My two years in Marks would be up in five months
and the defensive coordinator, Coach Johnson, was looking at accepting a job as the head coach at his alma mater,
Rosedale High School, forty miles away.

The next week, I drove up to Memphis and visited Coach
Holden. The left side of his body was gaunt and lifeless—
his spirit looked the same. I wanted to reach out to him
but I did not know what to do. Coach Holden would never
coach or teach at M.S. Palmer High School ever again.

Years later, Coach Holden is able to function well with a cane and coaches football at West Tallahatchie High School, southwest of Marks. He is a magnetic man who taught me a great deal, and I am forever in his debt.

CHAPTER 9

Students

When I first began teaching, I was a little nervous about meeting the students. They were from different sets of circumstances than I was. They spoke in ways I did not understand, and interacted in ways I could rarely relate to.

My fears were galvanized the first weekend of the school year, when a few of the school's students started a fire in the downtown stores of Marks, killing two white volunteer firemen. During my first week of teaching, we had a memorial service in a packed gym for the two firemen who lost their lives.

However, from that beginning in the quiet, somber gym, the compassion, innocence, and joy I found from my students slowly began to take hold.

Looking back on it, my fears were ultimately based on unfamiliarity and all the anxiety that can cause. The students of M.S. Palmer High School taught me innumerable lessons about the human spirit, which may have been difficult to learn if I had stayed in Colorado. I felt each student had a unique message to tell if only I had the time to listen. The protective emotional shells many of my students put on every time they walked into class were sometimes incredibly difficult to peal off. However, when students did reveal their vulnerabilities, their longings, and their personal stories, it was a tremendous transition that sparked real relationships.

From the classroom, to the athletic fields, and to the halls, there were so many students with so many stories that could break your heart or fill you with inspiration. I had a hard time keeping track of it all. I was inundated.

* * *

One of my students was a fifteen-year-old, charming and courteous, sophomore girl in my seventh period class who had a finer inner sense of manners and social etiquette than most adults. She was also one of those rare students whose academic curiosity ran deeper than simple grade achievement—a teacher's dream. However, she also had a building emotional thunderstorm inside of her that became obvious to anyone who bothered to look.

One day I ventured to ask her how she was doing outside of school. She told me that things had been pretty rough but she did not feel like talking about it. I honored her request but offered her the opportunity to talk to me if she ever felt like getting something off her chest. For the next few weeks, we never spoke about anything aside from typical classroom discussion.

Then, during a lull in classroom activity before the final school day bell rang, she approached me and confided that she had been sexually molested a number of times in her past and it was clear that her emotional scars were threatening to overwhelm her. Although the legal process surrounding the sexual abuse was over, the emotional wounds were still far from healed. I sat silently there at the desk beside her and listened as my mind tried to piece her painful words together. I felt I was way out of my league for strong, solid advice. It seemed listening and sympathy were my best two options. Later, I had her talk to a friend who had been through a similar experience. To this day, I do not know what the best course of action would have been. I was and am helpless.

* * *

Driving my players home from sports practice gave me the chance know my athletes on a more personal level than I ever could have expected in the classroom. One of my backs told me he was about to be a father. He told me he still talked to the mother of his child but was not sure if a long-term relationship would come out of it.

Perhaps a dumb question, I asked him how it happened. He told me that both he and his girlfriend were virgins but one night things were taken "too far." He told me it was the only time the two had ever had sex. Protection was an afterthought. Now he was not sure what to make of the whole situation but that he would do what he could to be a good father. I told him if he ever wanted to talk about it, I would be happy to. However, the subject was never brought up again.

* * *

There were also happy surprises. Victoria was a pretty sophomore in my second period social studies class who did well in all her classes. During her junior year, she was bumped up to regular-education classes. I asked her once what she had planned after high school. Victoria told me she wanted to be a fashion model. I told her that was a lofty goal and modeling is an incredibly competitive arena. I tried to make it clear that although it was good to go after her dreams, she should also have some backup plans.

Victoria told me that her modeling career had already started and her picture would be in *Vanity Fair* magazine in a couple months. I gave her a pleasant laugh and a pat on the back before I was saved by the bell. I thought either Victoria was lying, delusional, or a little of both. The last I heard, modeling agencies were not running through rural Quitman County looking for fresh talent on the catwalk.

A couple months later I was waiting in line with my groceries at the Kroger's in Clarksdale. A copy of *Vanity Fair* caught my eye. I grabbed a copy and thumbed through it. In the magazine, there was a fashion shot in the Mississippi Delta. The pictures presented an image of models dancing and listening to blues music over a catfish and barbeque along a bayou. Designer clothes adorned perfectly over the multi-ethnic beautiful people as they played the banjo and laughed into Delta air. It was an image I found no where in the Delta except these pictures.

Then on the last picture of the article, I found a photograph of a group of models standing with their arms around each other, smiling with their vibrantly white teeth. One of the faces in the back of the group portrait was none-other than Victoria. Needless to say, I bought the magazine and immediately transformed my distaste for the unrealistic glorification of the Mississippi Delta to pride in Victoria. I showed it off to all the students at school. I could not believe that a magazine like *Vanity Fair* would go to the Delta and a local girl would be photographed.

* * *

Victoria's little brother, Ralph, a freshman, was the classic introvert. During my first year of teaching, Ralph rarely spoke to me or other students in my class. He was short, slim and occasionally picked on for being quiet, respectful, and, as other students told me, a virgin.

Then during the second year, when I taught science and gave lessons on animals, he completely opened up to me. Although Ralph's reading and writing skills were at the second to third grade level, I have yet to meet a person who had such an instinctual love for zoology. During my planning periods, Ralph would come into my room with articles he had found on animals that he wanted to share with me or shows he had seen on the Discovery Channel. Ralph would sit and talk about topics like environmental degradation and its effects on endangered species and the realistic chances of genetic technology allowing scientists to bring back the Woolly Mammoths with viable DNA found in the frozen rock of Siberia.

Sometimes during my planning period when Ralph had gained his teacher's permission, he and I would walk out of the school building and look for animals we could identify with field guides. We looked in the trees, under wooden planks along the football field, or in the little ravine running through the campus. My time with Ralph will always be remembered not just as a teacher trying to provide a lesson to a student, but also as an outsider finding a friend.

* * *

Breanna was a student who had a crush on me and called me at home on several evenings during my first couple of months at the school. By coincidence, my jogging route went by Breanna's house and she would flag me down by jumping out the front door, calling my name. Her behavior in the classroom was loud, oblivious of discipline, and rude. Although there were days I could keep her behavior at bay, Breanna decided to really get me upset one October afternoon.

Breanna yelled. She pushed. She made fun of other students and me. I told her that her actions would quickly put her in the principal's office. Because I had yet to send a student to the office, she didn't believe me. She got out of her chair and ran around my room shouting. I chased her through the rows of desks. Before I could catch her, she grabbed a tape dispenser off my desk and rolled on the floor in the tape.

I gave a pass to one of my students and told him to get the principal. A couple minutes later, Breanna was carted off to the office. She was the first student I had sent to be paddled. However, her display continued with the principal, and the local police ultimately had to remove her from the school.

Breanna received a 10-day suspension. Although it was too long for any student to be out of school, I secretly was happy to have her gone as the class became far more productive and less stressful.

I talked to Breanna's mother a couple days after her suspension to discuss her behavior. Because my classroom was full of students for a physical education exam during my planning period, Breanna's mother and I squeezed into the tiny copy room adjacent to the library. As students and faculty walked in and out of the copy room for copies, I quietly asked Breanna's mother if there was a better approach to discipline than what I was able to come up with. I relayed that I was a new teacher and still was getting to know Breanna both as a student and as a person.

Initially, Breanna's mother responded with a long sigh. Then, after a few moments of silence, she said, "Now that there are all these laws against beating a child, I'm not sure what you can do with her."

I paused and then thanked her for coming out to the school to discuss this with me.

Later, I asked her sister, Crystal, what I could do to curb Breanna's misbehavior. Crystal just told me to hang in there and that Breanna would eventually come around.

During my second year of teaching, Breanna was doing a work study and I rarely saw her. However, when we did cross paths, she was always pleasant. She never called my house again. It was almost as if the horrible event from a year earlier had never happened. As I was finishing my two years of teaching, I saw Breanna walk up on the stage at graduation and receive her high school graduation certificate with a big smile on her face. I warmly smiled and clapped along with everyone else in the audience.

* * *

Rick was a student who was quiet and usually kept to himself in my fourth period class. Although his was in one of my smaller classes, our personal interaction was minimal. Then, strangely, about three months into my teaching, he was the first student to really open up to me. He told me he had gotten his girlfriend pregnant about two months before. The girlfriend and Rick were in a strained relationship and there was little communication. Rick told me that the best thing he felt he could do for the baby was leave school and start making money, perhaps at a fast food restaurant. Rick told me he wanted to do the right thing but recognized he had limited options. I was sympathetic to his plight and honored his ambitions to make money for the baby. I also told him that by receiving his degree, it would set a standard for his child. Our conversation was relatively brief, about fifteen minutes. I've no idea if it was because of our talk, but a year and a half later, Rick graduated from high school.

* * *

Sheena was a student I struggled to interact with. As a junior, Sheena could hardly read and spoke infrequently, even when called upon. My attempts always seemed to fail miserably. If I got a "Hi, Coach," it was a major victory. Then one day during a planning period, Sheena knocked on my door. I told her I was real glad to see her. My usual attempts at conversation went nowhere, but she took a board game from my shelf and set it down next to me. We played a few games of Connect Four. Although she was still almost entirely silent, she immensely loved playing the game. To my surprise, Sheena was very good and I rarely won. Sheena laughed, clapped her hands, and even gave me a high five. I think Sheena and I developed a friendship of sorts for that brief moment. It was not until a year and a half later that I knew how much she valued me. While I was on bus duty at the end of the school day, Sheena was walking by and she surprised me with a quick hug. It warmed my heart and I was the one who was speechless.

* * *

Kenneth was a very smart sophomore with a crippling speech impediment. Kenneth's inability to communicate frequently kept him quiet and made him the butt of innumerable cruel jokes by his classmates. Kenneth spent painstaking seconds gathering himself before the words left his mouth and they still regularly did not come out the way he had intended. Beyond this, Kenneth did not know how to properly spell his name. Kenneth spelled his name as simply "Kennth" without the second "e." When I told him that Kenneth had two "e's" in the name, he assured me that his mother told him that "Kennth" was the one and only way to spell it. After a couple months of failing to convince Kenneth, I had a run-in with Kenneth's mother. She confirmed to me that she had never heard of Kenneth with the second "e" but at this late date, Kenneth was sixteen years old, we should just go ahead and stick with "Kennth." Kennth and I did just that.

* * *

William was the classic trouble student. Loud, obnoxious, and clearly upset at the world, William would mark out his territory when he came into my room. Both creating havoc of his own and feeding off the mischief of others, William was a challenge. I tried to provide a positive atmosphere for William, but it frequently went amiss. He had a short attention span and could hardly get through a sentence without losing focus. Clearly not a strong reader, William was also very self-conscious about his abilities. Instead, William would spend hours perfecting his personal signature, varying its size and style almost endlessly. I felt, perhaps, that William believed if he could only get himself a new mind and environment, his talents and formal autograph would someday merge in importance and significance and his hours spent would not be wasted. Unfortunately, I never saw him come around the way I hoped and William acted the same throughout my two years of teaching.

* * *

Patrice was a strong student in my classroom. Always ahead on her work and willing to help others, she was the dream student. She had a baby before I arrived and truly had the maturity of a mother. She carried herself in ways that were well beyond her seventeen years. I felt having Patrice in the room was like having another adult with me. Patrice was probably the only student I talked to and confided in on an equal plane. I felt she deserved that. Sometimes, amidst the chaos, Patrice was an oasis of understandability and mutual respect.

* * *

Robert was a student I only had for seven weeks. I tried intensely to reach him—the stern approach, the affable friend, the kindly parent, and just being myself all failed. Every class turned into a power struggle between the two of us. Refusing to read, pay attention, or behave, Robert was a student who made a fifty minute class period feel an eternity. Robert showed no respect for my authority. He would get in my face, say horrible things about me, fold his arms, and dismiss me all in a few minutes. During a particularly bad day, and the last day I had Robert in my classroom, he threw crumpled paper at me while I was writing something on the chalkboard. I turned around and told him I would have to send him to the principal's office. Robert refused to leave his seat. I then had another teacher help me escort Robert out of the room. Robert never entered it again.

I often reflected about Robert's parenting versus my own, in an attempt to understand our differences.

Robert was the product of a one-night stand. He barely knew his mother and did not know his father at all. Growing up in poverty as an orphan, he realized his academic talents had clear limits at an early age and had no one to support him. I have a great deal of sympathy, even guilt, for Robert. His needs were larger than anyone could provide him in 50 minutes, five days a week. But as much as I wanted to reach out to him, there were other students in the classroom and I could not allow his behavior to interfere with their ability to get an education.

In contrast, my parents were high school sweethearts. They renewed their wedding vows on their 25th wedding anniversary on a beach in Hawaii. My two sisters and I grew up in a modestly affluent neighborhood in Loveland, Colorado. When I struggled in elementary school, my parents helped through everything. They gave support emotionally and financially through my every endeavor growing up.

I was later told that Robert did not handle male authority well, and it was best if I did not have him as a student. However, that was not the last time I interacted with Robert. About two weeks after he left my class, another teacher helped him write an apology letter to me. Robert folded the letter and handed it to me during a passing period. I read the letter, told him I was very thankful, and shook his hand. That was our last interaction.

* * *

The students of M.S. Palmer High School were perplexing, yet I felt I understood them better than any student body I had been a part of during my life. I admire and respect them, and I feel lucky to have been, briefly, a part of their lives.

CHAPTER 10

Meals from a
Vending Machine

The National School Lunch Program (NSLP) started in
the late 1940s during the Harry Truman administration,
and was then called the National School Lunch Act. Soon
thereafter, a free lunch program was set up for students
whose families fell under the poverty line. Today, a family
of four with an annual income of up to $22,945 can qualify
for free school meals, and families with incomes under
$32,653 qualify for a discounted rate. When I was a stu-
dent at Loveland High School, 12 percent of students had
free or reduced priced lunches.[18] At M.S. Palmer High School,
it was 98 percent who were eligible.[19]

At M.S. Palmer, the program also offered breakfast. This
usually consisted of a combination of biscuits, fruit, eggs,
pancakes, or sausage. The breakfasts were served in the
cafeteria in small white Styrofoam trays before school as
students came in off the bus.

At first glance, subsidized meals seemed like a nice deal every school day. However, as our Director of Food Services noted, the breakfast food was usually wasted and much of the budgeted money squandered. Many students neglected their free breakfasts for something that held far greater allure: the vending machines.

Many students chose vending machine food over tax-payer-provided breakfast. From the school's standpoint, the vending machines made financial sense. They produced decent profits, which could go to any number of deeply-needed school programs. A ten-minute break was added to the five-minute passing period before my third class. Any student hungry from not eating breakfast used this opportunity to buy vending machine snacks.

The vending machines served candy, Hostess pastries, and various flavors of Royal Crown soda. These sugary snacks had an almost hypnotic effect on my students. Although I knew sugar was something most children had great fondness for, I was taken aback by its dramatic appeal. Sugar had a charisma and pull that went almost beyond anything else.

Many of my students would do almost anything for candy, flocking to it like moths to a flame. Candy was frequently stolen from my desk. Candy could be used to curb misbehavior. If no candy was given before a test, my students demanded some. If a little bit of candy was given, they demanded more.

I tried to harness the effect for tests. I had once learned a little sucrose before an exam was good to perk one's mind for the concentration needed to do well so I bought small candies and handed them out before my tests. In addition to providing a tiny pre-test mental jumpstart, I felt the sweets would put students in a better mood, if they knew they would get candy out of the deal.

However, I found the vending machines came with a potential health hazard. I had many students who were so overweight they could no longer fit comfortably in their desks. Their girths bellowed over their desktops as they struggled to breathe. This usually led to students shifting their bodies so the notebooks were on one end of the desktop and their bodies on another creating an inconvenient position to write notes with. Also, this meant students could no longer sit in a desk the way it was designed, which prevented them from looking straight at me. Only after turning their heads at an angle were they able to make eye contact as I gave lessons. Mississippi is ranked 1st among states in obesity, and our vending machines were doing their part to contribute.

After that came lunch, which hosted its own set of problems. Lunch was a solid reality that no student or teacher could escape. Lunch at M.S. Palmer was anything but a temporary reprieve from the workday and an opportunity to have a meal with friends. Lunch, in many respects, was the most stressful and volatile moment of the day.

Over the span of an hour and a half, all 523 students of M.S. Palmer High School were expected to eat lunch in the small cafeteria that fit only around 80-100 students. A student on hall duty would knock on my classroom door, and I would line all of my students up single file for a walk down to the cafeteria. As classes crossed paths coming to and from the cafeteria, we teachers buckled down and made sure there was no jostling or that no loud talking erupted which would echo down the hallway. One of Rambo's many pet peeves was a loud class walking to lunch. The threat of his tongue lashing on a "can't-you-just-discipline-your-students-on-the-way-to-lunch" tirade was always imminent. Recognizing Rambo's hot-buttons with the teachers, some students spoke out or misbehaved on this tense walk to the cafeteria for no other reason than to get his or her teacher in trouble.

After successful navigation to the cafeteria, we all stood in a single-file line and awaited our food. Once the tray was in hand, we sat and ate with our students. On average, we had about six minutes to eat. Under the watchful eye of Assistant Principal Keys, who constantly checked his watch to make sure no one was eating for too long, we all ate in a mad rush. There was not time to talk or do anything but gorge our mouths full of food. Ironically, the quietest time for students was the actual act of eating lunch. Frequently, I was still trying to get a few bites out of my apple as I walked up to the trashcan to throw it away. Lunch was panicked and felt more like a feeding track meet than a meal.

After eating, I again navigated and managed behavior back to my classroom, hoping students' voices could be maintained as we walked by Principal Rambo's office. As my classroom door swung open and students filed back into my classroom, I took a sigh of relief. Like a warplane pilot's relief at successfully landing after a dangerous mission, I reveled that another lunch had effectively reached its end.

CHAPTER 11

SATP

I started taking the Iowa Test of Basic Skills (ITBS) early in elementary school, along with almost every student in America. I spent hours with a number-two pencil, a question booklet, and an answer sheet filled with tiny bubbles. Although they were not a part of our grades, the test could be agony—days of extensive, silent concentration with small breaks for water and the bathroom. When you saw the stacks of ITBS booklets on a teacher's desk, you knew you were in for a long day with little reward.

At MS Palmer, I found a test even more grueling than the ITBS of my childhood—the SATP (Subject Area Test Program). It included six separate sections: a writing assessment, narrative writing prompt, algebra test, biology test, English test, and history test.

A school district's stress surrounding SATP scores could not be understated. Score improvements meant greater funding for the school. The SATP tests were used as an accountability measuring stick to keep schools disciplined and a financial motivator for improvement. In Mississippi, there was a five point rating system for schools based on the SATP. Five-point schools were the best in the state, and one-point schools were the worst. A school that continued to deliver one-point ratings was at risk of losing local jurisdiction and falling into the state's control.

The year before I started teaching, Principal Rambo made a point to improve our SATP scores. He focused on remediation, taking time out of the normal school day to focus solely on preparing students for the upcoming SATP. During Rambo's first year, the remediation worked and our school rose from a one to a two rating.

A few months after I started teaching, a large banner was presented to the student body, stating M.S. Palmer was among the most-improved schools in the state for the SATP. Principal Rambo continually professed the urgency and necessity for our school to continue to improve on this most important test.

About a month and a half before the SATP, teachers were given review material for the tests. We designated time for remediation so we could teach students all the skills they would need to know to do well.

Special education students were not taking the exam because it was acknowledged that their scores would bring down the school average, compromising our school's ability to do well. During the remediation process, I helped teach SATP history information with other social studies teachers, leaving my special-education students with another teacher.

As the test date neared, Principal Rambo increasingly marketed its importance. After the previous year's improvement this test seemed a defining moment for the school.

When the test day arrived, I helped place all of the special education students in the gym with a couple of physical education teachers. Our singular goal was to keep everyone quiet so the test-taking students could concentrate.

The two physical education teachers brought paddles with them as a way to enforce discipline and maintain the desired silence. I had other ideas. On the second day, as the SATP continued, I brought in a television and two movies from my home collection: *Hercules* and *Star Wars*. I watched over the students as, in turn, the students watched the movies. The hours dragged by, but the two physical education teachers never showed their paddles again.

Since the SATP tests were so important for school funding, Rambo seemed willing to sacrifice a lot for the tests; but, in the end, SATP scores dropped slightly from the year before. Despite the school's increased efforts, our rating dropped from a 2.1 to a 1.9, enough to dock funding. Principal Rambo was not happy.

CHAPTER 12

A Queen

At Loveland High School, homecoming was usually regarded as a big deal—a unique opportunity for a nice dinner, a corsage, and a dance. Easy opponents were chosen for the home football game, there was a parade, and of course, the dance itself.

M.S. Palmer High School took it one step further. Students dressed to the nines with tuxedos, full dresses, corsages, styling gel, hair extensions and high heels. The homecoming court had more than twenty students, almost all of them seniors. In a spectacle of red and gold balloons and flowers, I remember walking by the girls of the homecoming court in the hallway and becoming enveloped in a cloud of dueling perfumes. The main events were the announcement of homecoming queen and, later that night, the football game.

During my second year of teaching, the young woman chosen was Latoya Minor. A beautiful honor student and one of the most honest, decent people I met in the Delta, Latoya was a rare gem at M.S. Palmer. Now, she was being honored by the entire school. During halftime of the football game, Latoya rode a float around the field, holding her tiara high. She glowed. Later that weekend, I can remember telling my mother on the phone that when I watched Latoya Minor wave at the applauding crowd, it was probably "the happiest moment in her life."

A week later we were on a four-day "Fall Break" weekend. I was driving to the school for our next football game. As the players put their pads on in the locker room, head coach Aaron Holden stood alone with his arms draped over the practice field fence, staring off into a bayou adjacent to the field. I walked up next to him and he did not say anything. After about thirty seconds of silence, he looked at me and said, "Why did it have to be her?"

Turning to Coach Holden curiously, "What do you mean?" I asked.

"Latoya Minor. She's dead," he responded. "Died last night." I was stunned.

He told me the story. The night before, Latoya was being taken home by her boyfriend, Bennie, our starting wide receiver. The Minors lived far out from other towns, as I'd learned driving Latoya's brother, Marlon, home from football practice. Long, dark, isolated, winding roads separated the Minors from other houses or towns. On one of these roads, a deer walked across the street and into Bennie's car lights. Bennie swerved to avoid the animal and rolled the car. Bennie was injured but managed to get himself and Latoya out of the car. Latoya was badly injured. By the time Bennie got her to the Minor house, she was dead.

The saying goes, "The good die young." I called home and told my mother that Latoya Minor was dead. Her reaction was the same as mine—silence.

CHAPTER 13

Deep Fried
Delta Livin'

Describing Quitman County to my Colorado friends was not easy. Usually I got responses like, "You sure went a long way from home." However, I think traveling to QC can best be measured in culture rather than miles—the state of Washington and Ohio are equally far away, but they feel far closer than the Delta.

There is a part of the Delta that seems like a time portal. The agricultural feel of the society, the more linear racial understandings, the greater emphasis on religious faith, and the small-town sense of community all resonate to a time before my birth. On the other hand, there were parts of QC I felt were far closer to who I am than Colorado or the other places I have lived. I remember driving along the causeways into New Orleans to see my sister run the Mardi Gras half-marathon. I was driving on Louisiana roads, with Mississippi license plates, listening to the band "Alabama" on the radio. I felt like a good ole' Southern Boy, and it felt good.

Food

One of my favorite southern details was, strangely enough, the meat. The local Supervalu grocery store had a meat department with ground beef, chicken, pork loins and all the meat I have grown to know and expect but it was also stocked with meats I did not know people ate: turkey necks, pig ears, fat slabs off the backs of pigs, pig snouts, pig tails, and chitlins (pig intestines, pronounced "shitlins," which do not make them sound any better). I brought in a Polaroid camera once and took a picture of the spread and sent it home to my parents to prove that I was not making this up.

Many of my students loved chitlings and on a dare, I told them I would have an order. On my way home from school I stopped off at the local restaurant, Peedee's Soul Food, and ordered the Chitlings Combo, which included coleslaw, french fries and a Coke. With plenty of hot sauce and a deep commitment to convince myself I wasn't eating what I was eating, they went down pretty easily.

Pigs' feet were also popular. They were the most expensive item on the M.S. Palmer concession stand menu at a $1.25, a whole quarter more than a hot dog. When my sister Heather visited me from Los Angeles, we went to a school basketball game. During the half-time intermission, Heather and I went to the concession stands. As I struggled to decide over peanut M & M's or a Twix candy bar to go with my Royal Crown soda, my sister's attention was absorbed by a little girl standing next to her, nibbling on a bright pink pig's foot she had just purchased. The grease of the foot made it difficult to handle and it fell on to the dusty hallway floor. The girl promptly picked up the foot and continued eating. I was intrigued—Heather was mortified.

Race

During a visit from my other sister, Haley, we had a run-in with Southern culture of a different color. On a bright, warm spring weekend morning, I thought I would take Haley on a drive around the county. As we drove to Lambert, two miles south of Marks, I passed a car going about fifteen miles under the speed limit. The black state patrolman quickly turned around and pulled me over.

I was feeling very confident that my driving was entirely legal. When I asked him what the problem was, he told me I merged too quickly. When I asked him what that meant, he tried to start a bitter argument with me, taunting me to get upset and get in bigger trouble than I apparently was already in. For a moment, I even felt he wanted me to get out of my car and start something. I struggled to stay calm and I took his ticket without any explanation of what I had done. When I pulled back onto the road, I turned to my sister and asked her what had just happened. Haley told me that I had done nothing at all and believed it was just an issue of race, clued in from his clear anger at me as much as the non-violation traffic ticket.

It was moment of mixed emotions for the black community I had immersed myself in. On one end, I felt incredibly empathetic to blacks, knowing that same experience had happened to them many times over the years. On the other end, I was very disgusted since I had just been castigated on purely racial terms myself.

Three weeks later, I took my students to another teacher so I could go to the county courthouse to address my traffic ticket, which was quickly dismissed.

Gambling

Gambling is another piece of the Delta puzzle. The casinos' glowing neon lights gave an odd contrast to the rich darkness of the rural night sky. The casinos were a double-edged sword for the Delta. The casinos do provide much needed revenue and jobs for the community but the prospect of gambling comes with its own set of liabilities as well.

Quitman County schools receive little financial return from property taxes and had to depend on Title I funds from the federal government. Much of the casinos' tax funds go to the public schools along the Mississippi River. QC, unfortunately, is one county removed from the river and thus does not host any casinos with the resulting funds to the schools. However, the 30 minute commute did not stop many Quitman County residents from working at casinos like Harrah's or Hollywood. In fact, when my students were asked what their dream jobs would be, many told me, "I want to work at the casinos."

However, no economically depressed area honestly wants its economic health dependent on gambling. At Harrah's casino in Tunica, you could play a free round of games if you deposited your paycheck there.

Kindness

Although I found the cultural oddities in food and casinos interesting, what I enjoyed the most was the kindness and generosity of the Delta people. I had never seen anything like it before in my life. The phrase "southern hospitality" was a clichéd term I grew up recognizing. However, it was something I attributed to films like *Gone with the Wind* rather than a reality. My experiences in the Delta changed all of that.

When I traveled to Marks for the first time, I knew no one there. I could only rely on the old high school friend of a friend of an acquaintance for temporary housing while I house hunted through the town.

As it turned out, that was all I needed. The Cassidys, were a white family who lived in Marks, were among the most genuinely friendly people I've met. They welcomed me into their home, fed me, and even did some of my laundry. The Cassidys maintained much of the cotton crop in the county and had a family heritage in the business. From endless home-cooked meals to social gatherings to talks about Ole' Miss football over a rum and Coke, the Cassidys stunned me with their hospitality.

Another family, the Rotenberrys, took me in as if I were kin. Shirley Rotenberry was the head chef at M.S. Palmer for decades and was always there for a hug and conversation. Shirley let me stay at her house and took me out for a catfish dinner several times when I returned from various weekend trips through the Delta.

If you could look past the poverty, a drive through Quitman County left you feeling good inside. People rarely hesitated to wave a hand or smile as my car treaded down the road. When my sisters came to visit me, they too, were struck by the friendliness of people. Somehow, as Colorado and many parts of the country followed the rat race of modernity, this essential component was left behind. I find myself waving to folks and smiling more easily at strangers in the Mississippi Delta than I do anywhere else.

The friendliness is also extended into conversation. Every time I went to the gas station, the post-office, or the grocery store, there were people there who knew me and were happy to talk. I loved those short conversations about what was going on at the school or my thoughts on this upcoming season's football team. It was comforting to feel a part of something like that. Although I had traveled so many miles from my Coloradoan home, family, and background, I never felt alone in the Delta.

Future Man

During my teaching years, I had a pet frog named Future Man, named after a character in the film *Bottlerocket*. Future Man was a small, unobtrusive pet, who required little maintenance. However, during the two-week Christmas break, he needed heat and water that I could not provide him while I was in Colorado. I put an advertisement on my chalkboard that if any student took the minimal care required to maintain Future Man, they would receive $20.

A large but gentle sophomore, Charles, approached me about the job. I sat Charles down and told him what little care it would require, but that I needed to trust him for those two weeks. Charles told me he felt he was more than up to the challenge.

Finally the semester came to an end and I had a flight out of Memphis only a few hours away. On this cold, overcast morning, I had everything packed in my car for my trip home. I drove over to Charles's house with Future Man in his aquarium. I walked up to the house and rang the door bell. Charles's sister answered the door and let my frog and me in. Once inside, Charles came out and I again told him what he needed to do. I shook Charles and his sister's hands, wished them a Merry Christmas, and started walking back to the car.

About ten feet from my car, I heard a loud voice yell out my name. Bounding out of the front screen door in a bathrobe, Charles's mother stomped across her front yard. My heart sank as she fearlessly walked toward me. Although Charles told me that taking care of my frog was fine with his family, I had not directly communicated with his mother about this.

For a couple of seconds, she stood there looking at me in a bathrobe too thin for both the weather and the open public. Before I had the chance to apologize for bringing a frog into her house, she said, "Coach Hoake, you better believe we will take good care of your Future Man. You just go have yourself a Merry Christmas." With that, I gave her a hug, got into my car, and started the first leg of my trip home for the holidays.

CHAPTER 14

A Christmas Story

When I was a child, Christmas time was a splendorous event. Following Thanksgiving weekend, Christmas season began with cartoons in the evenings: Frosty the Snowman, Charlie Brown finding sympathy for a forgotten Christmas tree, claymation Rudolph the Red- Nosed Reindeer, and the Grinch's feeble attempts at ruining the Whoville's celebration. We presented Christmas music performances at my elementary school. The local mall, stores, and streets all took on a glowing show with multi-colored light bulbs and decorations. My own home transformed with ornaments and grandeur. Cards from friends came in from across the country proclaiming Christmas greetings. The piles of gifts under the tree continued to climb, along with anticipation. The extended family united. Eggnog was passed around.

Now as an adult, I wanted to, in some small way, recreate that magical experience for my students. I went out to the local Fred's Convenience Store in Marks and bought ribbons, candy, and clear plastic bags. I put a mixture of candy in each bag and tied each with a big green-and-red ribbon. Each of my students was going to receive this surprise gift before we started the Christmas break. I could not wait to show each class that I went out and did something special for each of them.

On the last day of school before the Christmas break, I brought all the gifts and put them in my desk. When my first class arrived, we went through all the end of semester business and then I surprised them with my gifts. My students lit up with excitement, just as I had imagined. They were very thankful and we all wished each other a happy holiday. Initially, my plan was working perfectly.

However, an obvious point I failed to anticipate was that the latter classes would learn about the gifts from my first class. They were no longer surprised and were starting to demand their gifts immediately when they came into the room, rather than waiting until the end of the class. As the day progressed, students began coming up to me and asking if they could receive their candy now instead of waiting until class time. The situation was becoming increasing uncomfortable.

The final flaw to my gift-giving plan came during the time I needed to be in the hallway between classes so I could monitor hallway mischief. This meant I had a much more difficult time watching what was going on inside my classroom. At one point late in the day, while I was standing in the hall, I turned around into my classroom to find one of my senior students, Marcell, with his hand in my desk, fishing for Christmas gifts.

I yelled to Marcell to stop what he was doing. When I said this, Marcell grabbed a bag of candy, slammed my desk drawer shut, and folded the candy under his other arm.

I walked into my room and told Marcell that I saw him take a Christmas gift out of my desk. Marcell simply shook his head and said, "I don't know what you're talking about, Coach." I told him that I saw him do it with my own eyes not more than ten seconds before. At this point, I was sure he would give in and admit he did it but he just stared off and said again, "I don't know what you're talking about, Coach." I told Marcell that he could not possibly win this argument when I saw him take it and he was holding it in his hands. Marcell just folded his arms even tighter and refused to admit guilt.

It was about this time that I noticed that a red ribbon hung from his folded arms. I looked at Marcell for a third time in the eyes and asked him how he could possibly explain the ribbon dangling between the two of us. Incredibly, Marcell again touted his innocence. I ultimately had to have the principal come down and remove him.

After Marcell and the principal left, I started my class as usual. I tried to put the Marcell episode out of my mind.

Finally, as the class was winding down, Marcell re-entered the room. He had a slip from the principal's office, which read that he had been caught with theft and had been paddled. Marcell quietly sat in the back of the class. The class went on as usual.

After about ten minutes, Marcell raised his hand in the air to ask a question. I looked at Marcell and asked him what I could help him with. He stared at me and said, "Coach Hoake, what 'bout my candy?"

I told him that if he expected a Christmas gift thirty minutes after theft and lying, he was crazy. Marcell then got quite upset with me. "Ahh, Coach Hoake, you just way too hard on me! I don't want no candy no how!"

I told him I was sorry he felt that way.

As the class ended and students left for their two-week break, I told Marcell, "Merry Christmas." Marcell shook his head at me and said I was "nothin' but a bad man." With that, my Christmas holiday officially began. A Christmas story can take on many forms.

CHAPTER 15

Sexual Politics

I completed my Teach For America application right as the Bill Clinton-Monica Lewinsky scandal hit the press. My first semester in the Delta began as the impeachment hearings were getting underway. In hindsight, the irony is thick—Freud believed almost every human act can track itself back to a latent or overt sexual impulse. My time in Mississippi fell right in line with that belief.

A few days before I started teaching, Principal Rambo brought the five youngest male teachers into his office. It was clear that he had something very important he needed to speak with us about. We sat around his large desk anxiously awaiting his thoughts. Finally, when he felt he had our complete attention, Rambo told us, very seriously, that we were not to have sex with any of our students. Rambo said, "The girls at our school are wonderful young women. I have great pride for the girls here at the high school. However, some of them will try to tempt you. They will say things to you and maybe even grab you. You all need to be ready for this. I have been in education for over twenty years and I can tell you, I have never had sex with a student."

At the time, I felt our principal's lesson was superfluous. Of course you are not supposed to have sex with a student! This is a given, not a discussion that necessitated a debate. Not having sex with a student in twenty years of education should be the least common denominator, not cause for an award or a pat on the back.

A week later on the morning of my first day of school as a teacher, all the students sat in the gym bleachers. I stood in the hall, alongside the gym, peering through the window at all the high school students sitting there laughing, talking, and enjoying each others' company before another school year began. On the far side of the gym, I saw my fellow football coaches sitting on the stage in front of all the students. Without a second's thought, I walked across the gym in front of all of the students in the high school to join the coaches. The girls started to yell and scream at me with adulation. I was totally unprepared for this reaction. Not knowing what else to do, I put my hands over my head and did a "raise the roof" move which brought even more shrieks and shouts.

Shortly thereafter, the rest of the teachers joined us at the stage. Principal Rambo followed with a "get ready for the school year" motivational assembly. After the assembly, we broke into homerooms by teacher. I had a ninth grade homeroom with students with last names T-Z in the alphabet. I told my homeroom students that I was Coach Hach and they should follow me to my classroom. On the way from the gym, a girl in my homeroom told me, "Coach,

I will follow you anywhere." Perhaps Rambo's speech had not been so superfluous after all.

But despite the sexual energy that permeated the halls of M.S. Palmer, there was a lack of knowledge regarding the subject.

Our football practice field was the outfield for the baseball diamond and sat just outside a bayou. Animals of every sort were always crawling over. On this day, an adult wolf spider crept across the field while the players were in stretching lines as part of the pre-practice warm up. The wolf spider touched a player's hand. Startled, the player quickly stood up and pointed at the arachnid crawling across the grass. A ring of players encircled the giant spider, staring at it in wonderment. A coach came into the ring, stepped on it, and told everyone to get back to stretching.

Sammy, a (male) senior running back on the team, stared at the squashed spider laying in the grass and said, "Damn! That's the biggest spider I ever saw. That thing must be the size of my clitoris."

I laughed, put my arm around one of my fellow coaches and said, "Kids will say the darnedest things, won't they?" However, the spider situation revealed a troubling disconnect. With the teenage pregnancy rates that necessitated a Head Start nursery twenty feet from the high school and widespread venereal diseases, a lot less boasting and a lot more learning were essential.

CHAPTER 16

When Nature Calls

M.S. Palmer had the misfortune of sitting along a bayou, which housed a lot of native Mississippi wildlife. For some animals, the boundary between the bayou and the school was something of a grey line.

Before my first school year started, Principal Rambo brought the entire faculty together into the library for a motivational pep talk. He told us this was going to be a great year: the school was in excellent shape; we, the faculty, were ready to go; and the students were ours to enlighten. What Rambo failed to see, less than four feet behind him, was a mouse on the library book shelf staring at him through his entire speech.

One day during my planning period, I went to wash my hands in the teachers' lounge sink. I found not one, but two green tree frogs holding tightly with their suction cup fingers to the faucet. I picked both of them up, carried them out of the school. A student stopped me along the way and asked me what I was holding in each of my hands. I told him it was nothing to worry about. When I reached a little ravine near the school building, opened my clasped hands and the frogs' squirming moist green bodies sprang from my hands and into the water.

In my classroom, my desk housed at least one mouse. At least one mouse, I am sure of. Sometimes, when I opened my drawer at the start of the day, I would see a rodent dash out of the desk to a small hole in the bottom of my classroom wall. I tried to figure out how the mouse got into my desk, but I never found a hole. However, the impact of the mice was most acute with the ghastly odor they left behind. The smell of dropping and urine occasionally made me nauseous if my face was too close to the desk drawer when I opened it. Even though I made it a very strong point to clean the inside of my desk regularly, the odor always crept back.

And then there were the spiders. During a second period class once, an adult female wolf spider crawled across my classroom floor. Including her legs, she was about three or four inches long. In horror, my students got up and stood in the back of the class. I told one of my students to open the window so I could find a way to throw her outside.

I folded a piece of paper into a shovel and reached down to carry the spider to the window. Unfortunately, the moment the spider was on the paper, she immediately ran toward my hand to attack, so I shook her back onto the ground. I then tried to scoot her along the floor, edging her closer and closer to the window. Finally, she was in throwing range.

Now, I do not know enough about wolf spiders to sex them. However, I know it was a "she" because as she flew through the air out of my classroom, hundreds of tiny baby spiders came off her back and landed on the floor. My students mobilized to start stomping on the baby spiders, and an arachnid massacre ensued. But for weeks thereafter, baby spiders were common place, running along the floor and up and down my walls.

Insects were formidable foes for me in the Delta. I got up to work out every morning at 5:00 a.m. The weight room/ locker room was its own building, separate from the school and stood even closer to the bayou than the rest of the campus. The weight room was not heated, but seemed perpetually about five degrees warmer than the outside air. This little temperature differential was enough for many insects to seek the building as habitat.

During a bench press set of 270 pounds, a hornet dove at my head. Although not stung, my concentration was momentarily lost and I struggled to put the weight back on the rack. The hornet, called a "mud diver" in the Delta, was very protective of the weight room. Out of horror, I left the building altogether after another diving attack. I carried a can of *Raid* insect repellant when I went back to workout the next day and had it beside me during each set. I finally got the hornet and could continue my exercises.

The warm months of the school year also meant mosquitoes. They incessantly buzzed around my head and attached themselves to my arms and legs while I exercised. Eventually I just started lathering my body with *Off!* insect repellent before starting my morning workouts.

Another day in the weight room, I was lying on a small patch of carpet on the floor, stretching my hamstrings. An upside down football cleat sat on the floor next to me.

Suddenly, it started moving across the floor. It was 5:15 a.m and I had only been awake for about fifteen minutes and thought I might still be dreaming. I watched as the shoe slowly inched along the floor. I curiously picked up the cleat and found the largest water bug I had ever seen. I brushed him outside and went back to stretching.

Another workout day, a black widow spider, with its black body and red underbelly hourglass, walked up to my hand while I stretched. Because this is a very poisonous animal, I quickly put her outside by brushing her aside with a shoe.

The most dangerous encounter during my workout came toward the end of my first year of teaching. At 5:10 a.m., when I walked into the gym, it was always totally dark. The sun wasn't up, and the lights weren't on. When I flicked the light on, I found a cottonmouth snake coiled at my feet. The snake had probably come in searching for mice, which were commonplace in the weight room. Given that I was suddenly standing right over it, the snake lunged at me with its fangs and white mouth. I leaped into the air and yelled something profane as I dodged its bite.

I grabbed a broom and pushed the snake out of the open door and let it slither back into the bayou. It was one of the scariest moments of my life. Totally alone, I really don't know what I would have done if the snake had bitten me, because there wasn't a hospital for many miles. I got lucky.

CHAPTER 17

Hit the Gym

When I was in health class, I learned that humans have three generalized body types: ectomorphs are thin-boned and very slender; mesomorphs are larger-boned with a greater tendency for muscle mass; and endomorphs have a greater propensity to be heavy set. I knew right away I was an ectomorph. I was very conscious of how thin I was. I entered the seventh grade standing 5 feet 11 inches and weighing 112 pounds. When the basketball tryouts came around that year, an older and more muscled ninth grader jokingly told me that a string hung from my tank top, only to correct himself by saying that it was my arm.

Fueled by the motivation not to look like the guy in the Charles Atlas comic book ads who gets sand kicked in his face, I dedicated myself to lifting weights through high school and college. By my junior year of college, I started the football season at 6 feet 2 inches and weighing 205 pounds. I found a comfort in exercise. The stress of life always seemed more manageable and less important after a good workout.

After the conclusion of my senior football season in college, I continued to workout. My morning Mississippi workouts gave me a fresh respect for the day, no matter what obstacles might loom ahead.

The athletic director, Coach Holden, recognized my propensity to wake up early and work out. Soon after, Holden named me the school's strength and powerlifting coach. He told me the school never had a weight program before and it desperately needed one.

I was a little cautious at first, but a few weeks into the football season, I drafted a weight lifting routine that mirrored the program I did when I'd played. I started getting many of the football players into the field house after school for a couple of hours, helping out with techniques, spotting players with the weights, cleaning up the field house, and driving players home in my car. Many of our athletes had never lifted weights before and needed to be walked through the process. One of the players from my special education class actually put his shoulder pads and helmet on before he started lifting weights, believing it would help him. It was an uphill climb.

Coach Holden told me he was proud of the work I was doing, but that I needed to start thinking about my power lifting team. I was a bit gun shy because I'd never competed in powerlifting as a sport as Colorado did not have high school powerlifting teams. I just thought the sport was for the Olympics and late night strength contests on ESPN II.

We talked about the three exercises the athletes compete in and the rules that must be met. I then put a notice in the school announcements that we were starting a team and that anyone who was interested needed to stop by my room that week.

I think the student body was as dubious about powerlifting as I was. The interest was minimal. I had four competitors: three eighth graders and one junior, whom I naturally named team captain. We had no uniforms, so the boys came in street clothes or brought shorts. Because this was a winter sport and the field house had no heat, the weights frequently got very cold. Some of my athletes put old t-shirts around the metal barbells so they would not get frostbite on their hands. Many times my athletes could see their own breath in the weight room.

However, when the temperatures rose a few degrees, they started taking their shirts off and staring in the mirror, mesmerized by their physiques. One lifter, Ronald, would spend endless time thrilling at his growing muscles. I told him if he spent as much time concentrating on his exercises as he did ogling over his own body, he could probably win state. I noticed in the halls, my lifters were rolling up their sleeves and flexing at the girls in between classes. Although they worked pretty hard and enjoyed each other's company, I could not help thinking they joined the team for the wrong reasons.

It was trial and error the first season. We trained in the weight room for two months and then competed in our only meet of the year—the conference meet. My entire team could fit easily into my car as we headed off for Coffeeville, Mississippi, about two hours away. Through the winding wooded roads, my lifters were filled with anticipation for a meet we couldn't really visualize. My lifters chose the music selection during the trip, putting in a CD of a Mississippi group rapping "Shake dem Haters Off! Shake dem Haters Off!" This was a statement I had heard many times before by so many of my students. Again, it was the message of rising above the common circumstances of apathy and ineptitude. Now "Shake dem Haters Off!" was being used as a motivational mantra for my athletes as they braced themselves for their upcoming meet.

I parked my car in the Coffeeville High School parking lot next to the big school buses which brought droves of larger, stronger lifters. We slowly and nervously filed out of my Volkswagen and into the gym, overwhelmed by the size disparity of our competition.

At the meet, the conference powerlifting director told my team that we would have to pay to get into the meet, given we weren't affiliated with a high school. I explained to him that although we did not have school sweatpants or sweatshirts, we were the M.S. Palmer High School powerlifting team. Each of my athletes presented his M.S Palmer lifting singlet and the director then let us through.

Once in the gym, we were shocked by the size of the competition. My team seemed totally out of their league. Noticing their dropped jaws and huge eyeballs, I took them into the locker room. I told them I was proud of what they had accomplished over the past two months of training. I said they had seen pretty dramatic improvement and all they could do was their individual best.

My three eighth graders and junior had a tough afternoon. Although they tried hard, they were overwhelmed by the competition. I watched the meet nervously, hoping the day would not shatter their self-esteems. I watched as heavy weights were lifted, teetering in the air, and then dropped. The strained grimaces on my lifters' faces and the yells of their exertions rarely produced successful lifts. We looked like a middle school team that had showed up for the wrong meet. There were no parents of my athletes in attendance and I was their lone cheering section. Out of sympathy a couple of parents from other schools patted me on the back and told me I just needed to hang in there with my boys.

Finally, at the end of the day, the meet director grabbed a microphone and had each team stand up as he read point totals. He told everyone he would read the schools from least points to greatest to build anticipation. Our team was read first, with zero points. A number of people started laughing. The meet director jumped in on the microphone and said, "Hey, these guys deserve a hand, too!" Then, a couple distant claps sounded around the gym.

That evening, on the way home, I told my lifters I understood they were upset. I told them we were the youngest, smallest team at the meet. I also told them to remember this moment, because when we went back in a year's time, we would be very competitive.

At the end-of-the-year sports banquet about three months later, I got up to deliver a couple of powerlifting awards to my athletes, and told the audience that I really did not know what powerlifting was when I started the season. "I thought powerlifting was just a bunch of muscle-bound guys in skin-tight singlets grunting their way to a hernia surgery," I said.

A year passed and another powerlifting season was upon us. This time, more students knew about the sport and I had nine athletes: three seniors, one junior, one sophomore, three freshmen, and one eighth grader. I had athletes in almost every weight division. For this second

season, we had three months of training and four prelimi-
nary meets before the conference meet. I also told my lifters
we needed sweatpants and sweatshirts. I told them if they
would put down $20 a piece, I would pay for the rest of the
uniforms.

When I returned to Loveland for the Christmas holidays, my sister Haley and I went to an embroidery shop
and had uniforms made with "M.S. Palmer Powerlifting"
put on them. Unfortunately, however, my heavy-weight
lifter, Mario, was too big a size for the sizes the store offered. We went out to Target, ShopKo, and Wal-Mart, trying to find an XXXL pair of red sweat pants. Finally, in
K-mart's maternity section, we found the right size. We
ran back to the store and made our order. The money I
chipped in for the uniforms turned out to be a great investment, I got more out of it than I gave.

Two weeks later, a big box arrived at my door in Marks,
Mississippi. I brought the box to the field house and presented the sweats to my lifters.

As a team, we worked hard and became more competitive with each meet. I felt good about the direction my
team was moving. Finally, the conference meet was upon
us again. This time we had enough athletes to require a
small bus. We drove together to Senatobia High School in
northwest Mississippi. I told the team the same thing I
had the year before—all I asked was that they do their
individual best and I would be very proud of them.

The M.S. Palmer Powerlifting team competed hard and
well. Of my nine lifters, seven received medals for being
among the top three lifters by weight division in the district. One of my lifters, Sammy, won the whole conference.
A number of my boys' parents arrived and we had a cheer-

ing section. Even the parents from the other school who had patted me on the back a year before said this was a different team than the one they remembered. We had a celebratory dinner at McDonalds on our way home.

That evening, I drove to Memphis and saw Coach Holden, who was then in the hospital, recovering from his stroke. He told me he was proud of me and he wished he had been there. Strangely, a sport that I walked into with great reservation and caution turned out to be one of my most rewarding experiences at M.S. Palmer.

CHAPTER 18

School-land Security

Much of my time spent at M.S. Palmer was used trying to distance myself from the educational expectations I'd had previously. Teacher-student relationships, student outlooks on homework, interest in reading, and the work ethic of teachers and students alike were far different from what I'd experienced as a student in Loveland. However, after a year of separating myself, one evening brought Colorado schools back home to me in a truly tragic way.

Following a long day of teaching and coaching spring football practice, I came home to make dinner. Shortly after cooking a plate of spaghetti, I received a phone call from my sister, Heather. She told me it had been a very difficult day for her. I asked what had happened. Heather was shocked that I had not heard the news and told me about the incident at Columbine High School where two students massacred 12 fellow students and a teacher with hand guns and semi-automatic machine guns before taking their own lives. I was shocked. After a year of working in one of the poorest schools in the country, my own home state's public schools produced one of the most ruthless school occurrences ever. I could not make sense of it all.

The next day in class, one my students, Jimmy, rose his hand and asked, "Coach Hoake, you from Colorado, ain't you?"

"Yes, Jimmy, I sure am. Why do you ask?" I said.

"Well, Coach, why are those Colorado kids shooting at each other?" he asked.

As I struggled to find the appropriate words to respond, I looked out the window and saw a convict on the custodial staff mowing the grass on the side of the school. He was wearing his striped pants and white top on the hot, humid, Delta spring day, hard at work. It was a moment in which the world just was not making any sense.

I turned back to Jimmy and said, "That's a great question, Jimmy. I have no idea. I really don't."

At M.S. Palmer, we had frequent security check-ins. At the beginning of a check-in day, all my homeroom students took everything from their pockets and lay their school bags on the floor. A policeman would then walk through the room with a search dog. Usually, not much was found.

On one occasion, a gun was brought in. Apparently, an eighth grade boy admired the fish in a pond on his walk home, after being dropped off by the school bus, he decided shooting a gun at the fish would be pretty fun. That night he stole a gun from a local pawn shop and brought the gun to school the next day. It was found there, and he was suspended for ten days.

The most disturbing security issue affecting the school concerned a small group of kids, formed from among the few white students at the school. They got together and were making bombs with which to blow up the school. I do not know what the goal of blowing up the school was, but it never got very far. We knew the boys had gotten into a fertilizer plant and that bomb construction was underway. Principal Rambo kept us informed of the situation. *(See page 114.)*

I never took the bomb threat seriously. I saw it as a few high school students trying to pull a prank. I even had one of the students, Johnny, in my classroom. He looked somewhat isolated and insecure, but I saw nothing within him that displayed malice. So, although some wanted to bomb the building, and I broke up fights and occasionally got my face in the way of an errant punch, I never felt threatened at M.S. Palmer. Weapons were something I never came across. Massacres like the one at Columbine never seemed a potential reality in Marks.

MADISON S. PALMER HIGH SCHOOL
MR. ROOSEVELT RAMSEY, PRINCIPAL

November 12, 1999

To All Teachers:

Please be on alert, I have received a threaten note that says three white boys will blow some portion of the school up today. It may be a hoax or it may be serious. We will treat it as being serious. Please be watchful. I will keep you informed.

Sincerely,

Bomb threat notice from Principal Rambo.

CHAPTER 19

Two Religions

In the weeks following my college graduation, I was at a dinner party with my parents. A friend of theirs asked what plans I had, now that I was done with school. I told him I was going to teach in the Mississippi Delta, and he said, "The Deep South, huh? You know, they have two religions down there. One of them is the Baptists, and the other is college football. Depending on the time of year, one will take precedent over the other."

I assumed he was exaggerating and we laughed as we drank our glasses of wine. Only after getting to Mississippi did I realize he was right. Christianity and college football bled with a tradition, honor, and pride that nourished the Delta.

As a high school football coach, I could call the Ole Miss athletic front desk and garner free tickets to any home game I wanted. I took full advantage. I had always loved football and played for twelve years, including, playing all four years during college. I had been to Denver Bronco games and my dad and I had season tickets to the Colorado State University Rams, but I don't think I ever recognized football's full potential until I ventured into Oxford, Mississippi on game day.

The pillared campus was beautiful during a home game. Nestled just outside of Hugh-Vaught Stadium was the Grove, an on-campus meadow that hosted the largest tailgating party I had ever seen. The tailgating started mid-week and slowly built momentum toward kickoff. Blue and red were everywhere, surrounded by the smell of appetizers and beer. And when game day finally arrived, people dressed for it. Fraternity undergrads with shaggy hair cuts wore ties, and beautiful coeds wore spring dresses, fresh from sorority row. It was an environment that almost took my breath away.

The wonderful game-day Ole Miss verse still tugs at my heart.

> *Hotty, totty, gosh all mighty,*
> *Who the hell are we? Hey!*
> *Flim, flam, bim, bam,*
> *Ole Miss by damn!*

South Eastern Conference (SEC) football was unlike anything I knew. It had an almost seductive quality I didn't find anywhere else in sports. I learned to make heroes of the national championship teams of the late 1950's and early 1960's. I revered Manning quarterbacks, and the phenomenal running back Deuce McCallister. And I found myself disliking teams like the Alabama Crimson Tide, LSU Tigers, Arkansas Razorbacks, and those darn boys over in Starkville, the Mississippi State Bulldogs, who we played every Thanksgiving in the Egg Bowl.

However, my most striking memory of Ole Miss rival loathing came from the Auburn Tigers, and the person who exposed the disgust for Auburn was, incredibly, my own mother.

My first year in Mississippi, Tommy Tuberville was the Ole Miss head coach. Tuberville had taken the team out of the cellar and the scrutinizing eye of NCAA probation and had given the program respectability again. Ole Miss was once again a winning team, and Tuberville was loved as Oxford's favorite son.

However, just after the Egg Bowl in 1998, Tuberville left Ole Miss to coach the Auburn Tigers. He didn't tell anyone in the community, or on his team, of his decision. In an instant, Tuberville went from the crowned prince to the most hated man in Lafayette County. During the spring of 1999, the billboards in Oxford read, "123 days till Memphis, 144 till Tuberville." Each day, someone changed the number of days until the opening game of the season and the big showdown against Auburn.

And here's where my mother fits in. My parents came down to visit me for a fall weekend. They went to my high school game on Friday night, and we decided to visit Oxford on Saturday. It just so happened to be the same weekend as the Ole Miss- Auburn game.

This was an away game for Ole Miss, and Oxford was essentially a ghost town. The Square, a collection of quaint shops and probably the most popular place in Oxford, was vacant. The statue of the Confederate soldier, standing in the center of the Square, had no admirers on this eerily quiet afternoon.

My parents and I went into a sports bar to eat lunch and watch the game. It was very competitive and the game went into overtime. The Ole Miss fans gathered around the television like wasps to a nest, chanting "Hotty Totty," the whole way.

In the end, the Auburn kicker lined up for an easy field goal to win the game for the Tigers. But the kick sailed wide right, and Ole Miss had beaten their old coach, Tuberville. The place went wild. The "Hotty Totty" chant bounced off the walls. On the television screen, the Auburn kicker sank his head in his lap, obviously crying.

My mother said, loud enough for those around her to hear, "Oh, I just feel so sorry for that poor kicker."

The bartender narrowed his eyes as he looked at my mom and said, "Well, it looks like we got ourselves an Auburn fan."

My mom, who had no affiliation with the Auburn Tigers, tried to temper the growing hostility and said, "Oh no, I'm from Colorado."

The bartender then said in an even louder voice, "Well, it looks like we got ourselves a Yankee Auburn fan." I can't think of a more vile way of describing a human being in Oxford. We quickly paid our bill and walked back out into the brilliant sunshine in the Oxford Square. Running through the street was a college student waving an Ole Miss flag.

∗ ∗ ∗

The other religion in Mississippi is Christianity. If the Deep South is the Bible Belt, then Mississippi is its buckle. Christianity permeated everything.

I grew up in a religiously liberal family. I remember a story my father once told me about a time he attended his Lutheran church in Iowa. During Sunday school class as a child, he once asked his teacher if his pet cat, "White Kitty," was going to heaven after it died. The Sunday school teacher became very upset with my father and scolded him in front of the class for asking such a blasphemous question. My father felt humiliated. Although my father is a very ethical and intensely spiritual man, he found his innate curiosity unwelcome in his formal church upbringing. My mother, on the other hand, found a wonderful community at her Presbyterian church growing up in the same small town in Iowa. However, she found the religious practices of her parents too severe, with love overshadowed by a dictatorial faith stymied in rules.

My mother attempted to show us the kind of community she had growing up, minus the overemphasis on rules, by taking us to a Presbyterian church for a few years when I was child. Somehow, though, it never quite caught on and we stopped going. So for me, strict religious observance always played a very secondary role in my life. However, in Quitman County things were certainly very different.

Just days after arriving in Marks, a man stopped me in the Supervalu grocery store. In such a small town, as a newcomer, I was clearly an unfamiliar face. The man did not ask who I was and how I was doing. Instead, he simply asked me what church I was attending. I told him I didn't have one and he frowned, shook his head and told me it was time I found one.

Later in the year, I was out running on a Sunday morning. After all the craziness of the school week, it was just what I needed. The birds were chirping, the sun was warm, the trees were green, and the sky was blue. I picked up a couple turtles trying to cross the road and carefully carried them to the other side. I ran shirtless. If a spiritual experience existed, I felt, this must be it.

During the run, a man drove by me and stopped the car. It took a few seconds for the dust to settle behind his wheels. The driver, an obese black man, lowered his driver side window to talk to me. He was smoking, and clouds of smoke rose from the open car window. "Young man, it's Sunday mornin'. Shouldn't you be in church right now?" I didn't know how to respond, and he drove off.

Even M.S. Palmer—a public school—followed suit. Assemblies and sports events always set aside time for the Lord with public prayers.

In addition, many of my fellow teachers were very up front about their religion in the school setting. A math teacher always told me he was having a blessed or glorious day because of what the Lord had given him and he always had a Bible for everyone to see on his desk.

Another teacher told me he was concerned my priorities were too wrapped in pleasures of the flesh and not in line with the Lord. I worked out five days a week, both in the weight room and running on the streets. The teacher felt I was too consumed with exercise and the potential worldly vanity that accompanies it. He went on to show me Biblical verses that supported his argument (I've always been uncomfortable with people who give unsolicited religious advice, and this instance was no exception.

In another instance, I once asked a fellow special education teacher (and pastor) where he felt the dinosaurs existed in the Bible. He responded by telling me he felt dinosaurs existed during the Middle Ages when people with swords slashed dragons. I didn't tell him that a few doors down I was teaching that dinosaurs and man were separated by 65 million years of evolution. Instead, I shook his hand and told him I appreciated his time and thoughts.

Even some of my students questioned my salvation— some of the more disruptive students felt discipline from a non-churchgoer was immoral.

However, despite some obvious grievances, I also saw great hope and promise come out of the church.

For example, when my powerlifters approached me to request a team prayer before each meet, I told them if this was the team's desire, they had my full support. When we prayed, I saw the strength of their faith and the focus they found.

I even attended church on occasion. For a brief time, a Baptist minister in training lived with me to share rent. To offer support, I attended a couple services when he gave sermons. After that, I attended church more frequently, and started going to the First Baptist Church in Marks. This was a white church, which gave me a unique opportunity to spend time with the white people in town. Everyone was wonderful to me. There were always handshakes, good wishes, and smiles. I really did feel my mother's sense of community in that church.

In all, a relationship with Christ gave so many wonderful people a sense of boundary, optimism, and hope. I would not change a single thing about the Delta's love and faith for Christ. Faith gave Mississippi the humanity and the uniqueness that made it the home I loved.

CHAPTER 20

Janice

The academic life of a special education teacher and student was more than time spent in the classroom. Sometimes, outings took us away from the school. These events were usually received with open arms because they broke up the school days and gave students a much needed change of scenery.

For example, on one spring day, a local community college hosted a multi-county-wide arts and entertainment presentation for special needs students. The students loaded onto the bus and we drove 45 miles for the big event. We filed into the basketball gym stands and got ourselves ready for the display, which grayed the line between education and a circus. We all watched as a Memphis blues singer sang "Old Man River," followed by three police men (still wearing sidearms) singing songs to a tarantella beat. Then the North Mississippi Special Needs Beauty Queen was given a tiara and flowers, and the performance ended with clowns, mascots, balloons and noises.

Afterwards, the students had the chance to walk down to the gym floor and participate in a number of arts and crafts as well as taste a multitude of sugary treats. This was a feel-good event that lasted much of the school day.

However, as much as the students enjoyed that day, the big end-of-the-year event was the day at Lake Enid about 35 miles northeast of Marks. This was an annual occasion to get outside into the warm air and enjoy each other's company outside of the confines of school. Lake Enid hosted a large park and beach that gave our students the opportunity to be kids again, if only for an afternoon.

The celebration at the end of my first teaching year, came on a warm Friday in May. After the most challenging year of my life, I too, felt this warm spring day was a perfect reprieve. I sat in the bus, along with my students, peacefully enjoying the scenery of the rural roads as we drove along the countryside toward the lake.

Not long after getting off the bus, the other teachers began preparing the barbeque for lunch while I accompanied a number of students down to the lake as an unofficial lifeguard. I was surprised to find many of the students were fearful of the water and could not swim. None of the students went more than three feet deep. In the shallow end, I showed a few students how to stroke their arms. Everything was going fine. Then I turned around.

In no more than two-and-a-half feet of water, a junior named Janice lay unconscious, face down, completely submerged. My heart sank in terror. I grabbed her by the shoulders and began dragging her to the shore. For the ten longest seconds of my life, I sat in the sand, trying to think how to help. Janice's sandy, frozen face stared back at mine. Just as I was about to start what I remembered of CPR, she began to move. She started to cough and spit water out her mouth and nose. When she had enough strength to stop coughing, she began to panic. Janice was momentarily stunned and had forgotten where she was. I tried to keep her calm by telling her that she was alright and she just needed to rest. "Thank God," I thought to myself. With no other adults within a shout's distance this was, perhaps, the scariest moment of my life.

After letting Janice rest for a couple minutes on the beach, I helped her up. I walked her to a park bench where she could sit and look out at the lake. Janice was crying and she told me that this had happened a couple times before—she'd slip on the sand and fall under. "Oh, Coach Hoake, I am so sorry," she said over and over again.

Making sure no one else got back in the water, Janice and I walked arm in arm around the park. We talked about swimming, school, our families, and life. She slowly calmed down and we joined the rest of the students.

I told the other teachers that there was a swimming incident with Janice but that we were both okay. The rest of day at the beach went on as usual, but I was shaken.

The next week, Janice stopped by my classroom to thank me. A year later, Janice graduated from M.S. Palmer. I was certainly happy to see her in her cap and gown, walking up the stage to get her diploma.

I hadn't spoken to Janice before that incident, and we didn't speak much after that day, either. However, we shared one of the most powerful moments in perhaps both of our lives.

CHAPTER 21

Finding My Cay

A couple days after I had completed my teaching at M.S. Palmer, after I had put my supplies away and taken down all the posters in my classroom, I took a walk around the school, reminiscing about my two years. I stopped at the library and walked among the books, looking at the various titles. One book caught my eye: Theodore Taylor's *The Cay*—a book read to me, and my whole class, when I was in the sixth grade by my teacher Sara Terrell. As a 12 year old at that time, I loved having this book read to me. Using her best Dutch and Caribbean accents, Ms. Terrell made the book come to life, allowing me to momentarily forget about my preoccupation with sports, initial inkling thoughts about girls, or that I was even at school at all.

At that time, Ms. Terrell was just out of college. She has since gotten married and had changed her name but I will always remember her as Ms. Terrell. Now I was in her shoes as a new teacher with only two years experience out of college.

I grabbed *The Cay* off the library shelf and brought it back to my classroom. Sitting in my desk in a now empty and strangely quiet classroom, I poured through the book, remembering the way Ms. Terrell read it.

Here is the story: A young boy named Phillip lives on the Dutch island of Curacao, just off the coast of Venezuela during World War II. Forced to flee his home due to German encroachment, he and his mother take a ship bound for Miami. Phillip's ship is hit by a German torpedo, killing most of the passengers, separating him from his mother. Phillip ends up on a small, isolated Caribbean island alone with another survivor, a large, old, black man named Timothy. Further, Phillip had hit his head on a piece of timber while abandoning the ship and is temporarily blind. On the cay, Phillip and Timothy initially interact with great caution but ultimately become immensely close friends. After many adventures, a hurricane hits the small island and Timothy is killed. Shortly thereafter, Phillip is rescued. Phillip finally reunites with his family and receives three operations to repair ocular nerves, bringing back his sight. At the end of the book, Phillip imagines going back to the cay to rehash his fond memories with Timothy. Ms. Terrell concluded *The Cay* by reading, "Maybe I won't know it by sight, but when I go ashore and close my eyes, I'll know this was our own cay. I'll walk along the east beach and out to the reef. I'll go up to the hill to the row of palm trees and stand by his grave. I'll say, 'Dis b'dat outrageous cay, eh, Timothy?'"[20]

I remember, sitting in my desk as sixth grader as Ms. Terrell finished the book, wishing that I, too, had a similar experience on a cay. Though I hadn't realized it until it was over, I did—and it was Quitman County.

In Quitman County. I will always remember walking into my classroom in the early morning, before the fog lifted over the bayou outside my window. I will always remember believing I was driving my car through the rain, only to realize that I was passing through thousands of flying insects. I will always remember the taste of the Crawdad Delight pasta dish at the Venice Pizza Company in Oxford. I will always remember my students huddled on the floor of the hallway during tornado warnings, waiting for updates from Mr. Keys over the loud speaker, on the twister's location. I will always remember Coach Holden strutting across the football field at the end of practice, as the sun went down over the trees.

Someday, many years from now, when I am an old man, I will drive down into the Mississippi Delta along levied roads that feel like causeways over a white ocean of cotton toward Quitman County and M.S. Palmer High School. When I arrive, after the school day is done, I will go into my old classroom. I will look at the desks and remember the faces staring back at me and in my mind I will always be Coach Hoake.

Shake
dem Haters Off

Years have passed since living in Marks, Mississippi as a teacher and coach at M.S. Palmer High School. In 2004, I returned to the northern front range of Colorado, to serve as the executive director for a non-profit organization dedicated to promoting science education. I find myself falling back into many of the same routines of life and conversations I had before I left for the Delta. I take lunch breaks at the local restaurants like Chili's, Souper Salad, and Applebee's Neighborhood Bar and Grill, which are plush with Loveland High School sports regalia on the walls. I work out in a mega health club with four indoor tennis courts, endless exercise machines and weights with two pools, and take advantage of the newly finished larger-than-life outlet mall for my holiday shopping. I eventually became the member of a local progressive Christian church.

The Mississippi years have begun to feel strangely distant, like an experience from another life.

In the end, although I saw and experienced what my students were going through, I never really was a part of it. At least, I did not experience it as they did. For me, there was always an escape hatch. At any time, I could walk away from the little town of Marks in so many literal and fundamental ways that my students and community could not. Even when my students and I were struggling together day in and day out with reading and discipline, we both knew this was the case.

I sometimes wondered if I would have taught my classes differently if I had grown up in Marks. How would I have communicated and relayed the world to my students if I had indeed "shaken dem haters off" when I was in high school there at M.S. Palmer, got a college education, and came back to Marks to teach the students? Would the students have respected me more? Would they have listened to my every word with greater authority? Would I have been a greater role model?

When I was a high school student, I did not "shake dem haters off" because I did not have to. I did not grow up in an impoverished corner of our country and my personal childhood did not have to face, or even really need to acknowledge, the challenges the majority of my students faced.

My students knew I did not "shake dem haters off" when I was their age and I probably felt that I could not have if I were in their shoes. I was just a person who reflected my fortunate upbringing as they reflected theirs.

When I finished college from an elite private school and went off to teach in one of the most impoverished parts of our country, I naively felt that by sincere motivation and self-appointed charisma, I could reverse the circumstances of my students' lives. During those two years of teaching I realized that in almost all of the fundamental ways that mattered, I could not. It was incredibly humbling.

Looking objectively, I was a competent teacher but certainly not a brilliant one. I worked at it hard. I think I made a positive difference but I am not sure to what degree. Regardless, that degree of difference, no matter how minute, made the experience worth the effort. Selfishly, I gained immensely from the experience.

I realized that teachers and schools do not exercise an over-arching influence on students' lives the way many of us wished they would. Frequently, they serve as sponges for all their respective communities' successes and failures. If a community has a lot of financial security and supportive families, the school will succeed. If a community is impoverished and family support is minimal, the school will most assuredly fail. Schools and teachers contribute to its communities' students behavior, character, and education but only as a part of a much larger system.

Teaching is one of society's most challenging careers because you are asked to take responsibility for a wide array of conditions that are completely beyond your control. I thought I would have more control being in front of the classroom than I did. Anyone who can master teaching, who can master communicating and empathizing with young people in ways that both educate and empower them, despite the background the student brings into the classroom, is someone who deserves our society's greatest respect—as much respect as any doctor, politician, lawyer, celebrity, athlete, minister, artist, anyone, really.

Renowned 19th century writer, Fyodor Mikhailovich Dostoevsky, said that, "The degree of civilization in a society can be judged by entering its prisons." Personally, I think it's by entering our schools.

Endnotes

1 Exhibit: "Separate is Not Equal: Brown v. Board of Education": National Museum of American History, Washington DC.

2 Isserman, Maurice and Kazin, Michael, *America Divided* (New York: Oxford University Press, 2000) pp. 36

3 Story of the Death of Bessie Smith: http://www.lewrockwell.com/orig/jarvis6.html

4 2000 Mississippi census: http://quickfacts.census.gov/qfd/states/28000.html

5 Study on the Mississippi Delta using 2000 census data: http://quickfacts.census.gov/qfd/states/28000.html

6 Website regarding Lyndon B. Johnson's role in the Civil Rights Movement: http://www.historylearningsite.co.uk/Lyndon_Baines_Johnson.htm and http://usinfo.state.gov/usa/infousa/facts/democrac/40.htm

7 Cobb, James. The Most Southern Place on Earth: The Mississippi Delta and the Roots of Regional Identity (New York, 1992), pp VII.

8 http://quickfacts.census.gov/qfd/states/28/28119.html

9 *The Quitman County Democrat*. Vol. 97, No. 45, March 18, 2004 pp 1.

10 http://www.segenealogy.com/mississippi/ms_county/qu.htm

11 http://wwwsegenealogy.com/mississippi/ms_county/qu.htm

12 *The Quitman County Democrat*. July, 1964.

13 Cobb, *The Most Southern Place On Earth*, pp. 238

14 Cobb, *The Most Southern Place On Earth*, pp. 324

15 The Jackson, Mississippi newspaper, http://www.clarionledger.com/news/9912/23/23delta.html

16 http://ncrve.berkeley.edu/CW73/ShowcaseSchools.html

17 http://www.greatschools.net/modperl/browse_school/ms/804/

18 http://ncrve.berkeley.edu/CW73/ShowcaseSchools.html

19 http://www.greatschools.net/modperl/browse_school/ms/804/

20 Taylor, Theodore. *The Cay*. (Garden City: Double Day and Company, Inc., 1969) pp. 137.

CPSIA information can be obtained
at www.ICGtesting.com
Printed in the USA
LVOW10s0309171116

513337LV00001B/97/P